AN
AFRICAN
MEDITATION

by

V. O. AWOSIKA

An Exposition–University Book

EXPOSITION PRESS
New York

EXPOSITION PRESS INC.

50 Jericho Turnpike   Jericho, New York 11753

SECOND EDITION

LIBRARY OF CONGRESS CATALOG CARD NUMBER: 69-17226

EP 46908

Dedicated to the most cherished memory of my loving parents

Rt. Rev. Bishop D. O. Awosika, M.A., L.Th.
1893–1965

Alice Remilekun Awosika
1905-1962

Preface

I have found it worthwhile to compile this book as a monument to the various discussions, inspirations and reflections that I experienced during my stay in England. My hope and belief is that this book will contribute to mutual understanding and healthy relations between the peoples of European descent and those of African descent in all lands; and that it will help in setting a solid foundation on which their future generations will probably need to build. The tenor throughout has been to provoke thought rather than to attempt to answer difficult if not impossible questions.

I wish to express my gratitude to Miss Penelope Thompson and Miss Margaret Magee, both of Oxford, England, for their patience and kindness in typing from an almost impossible handwriting; and to Mr. Samuel Abidakun for his indefatigable performance throughout the formative stage of this book until the moment the first edition came out.

Lagos, 1968

Contents

AN
AFRICAN
MEDITATION

CHAPTER ONE

The Universal Human Brotherhood

Man is characterized by his excessive desire to survive. Superimposed upon this are his endless pursuits of comfort, convenience
and security. In his obsession to survive and feel secure in his
environment he comes into competition with others. He develops
will and his ambition. He strives hard to attain power, and he
would wield it as he pleases. Often, not stopping at ensuring
his security, he aspires to prevail upon and dominate others.
The elements of power include those which are inborn,
forming part of the individual's personality: his personal charm,
physique, wit and intelligence; and those which are acquired,
out of economic, social, religious and other spheres of human
endeavor. In modern life the most effective and obvious form of
power is that wielded by the head of government in any country.
Every person is sometimes fascinated, albeit whimsically, by
each form of power. Most people see something inherently good
in almost any form of power, in being acclaimed in the superlative for the various sorts of performance of which a human being
is capable, the more frequently when these are noble. But none
of these powers is ever absolute. One only has to have been a
head of state or government for a few minutes before he realizes
how much he envies others who wield certain other types of
power which he does not.
Human commitment to the cause of peace can be accepted
as a basic instinct. Indeed, certain leading authorities on human

behavior postulate that crime is a departure from the norm for which the individual should neither be held fully responsible nor punished. The instincts for peace and for fellowship, together, form the basis for universal human brotherhood.

The universal endeavor for peace, in its most basic and utopian meaning, calls for an instance in which order, justice and fair play attain perfection. It is no surprise, therefore, that attempts have always been made, in one way or another, to advocate and even to achieve a world government which would foster a universal sense of belonging together. These attempts have never been convincingly successful. Instead, there are proliferations founded on artificial territorial boundaries and on history, race or ethnic groupings; others are founded on economic, religious and cultural grounds—the phenomenon of nations often acutely conscious of one another's existence. So far in human history the United Nations Organization has come nearest to providing a kind of universal central government, even when it bars the admission of 700 million Chinese.

Whenever any threat is directed at man's survival, the delicate balance of peace is disturbed. Suspicion, enmity, violence and war then become increasingly inevitable. The instinct for survival is the root cause of sporadic armed conflicts, animosities and apprehensions among the nations and peoples of the world.

To ensure his survival, man seeks protection beyond himself. He seeks to cooperate with others. Instinctively he recognizes his kith and kin within the compass of universal human brotherhood. Throughout his existence he is almost incurably conscious of the group to which he belongs. He finds it effortless, safer and even natural to be with that group and would cast his lot with it rather than with any other. Thus he recognizes his blood brothers and his neighbors. He recognizes those with whom he shares a common survival and a common destiny. He recognizes those with whom he shares common interests and ideals, and dedication to definite causes, such as the advancement of peace, science, literature, music, sports, entertainment. The significance he would attach to each one of these bonds depends considerably on the challenges that are implicit in the given environment. Of supreme importance are those which would jeopardize his physical, social or economic existence.

Ultimately man would admit that everyone is his kith and kin. "We are all one." And indeed, all kinds of beings—the germ, the ant, the whale—are all deserving of his brotherhood and his sympathy simply because they possess *life* in common with him.

Those who find a common need for ensuring or enriching their survival, or even for surviving at all, are drawn almost inexorably toward collaboration and unity of purpose.

In the second half of the twentieth century the African skin typifies that inescapable uniform which denotes a common identity of kith and kin who have been abused, misused and pommeled, not so much for their creeds, beliefs, ideals or pursuits, nor indeed for any crime, nor because of their dark skin, but deep-rootedly because of the resourcefulness of the continent they inhabit as their birthright and their God-given land.

In our age the world has been shrunk immeasurably by phenomenal achievements in science and technology. The necessity and the demand for universal human brotherhood have attained an unprecedented pitch. The lunatic and suicidal element in war has become more apparent than ever before.

Whereas the general trend is toward closer international and interracial cooperation, or should we say, toward internationalism and interracialism, there are still the opposing forces of national and racial consciousness which harden as ignorance is dispelled and the different nations and races become increasingly conscious of themselves and of others, even when they are located continents apart.

The debut of Africa on the world stage after emergence from the stultifying mud and swamp of colonial tutelage remains one of the most significant turning points in the history of man.

Now, in at least four continents, the peoples (or their descendants) of Europe and of Africa are joint occupants, in functional contact and explosive embrace with each other. These two racially most polarized and distinct peoples are also among those who represent the two extremes of human survival. On the one hand are those of European descent who not only enjoy the highest standard of living, social exuberance and economic abundance ever known to man on earth but whose lead in man's endeavor to defeat his environment has become eminently unchallenged if not unchallengeable. On the other hand are the people of African descent who, largely through the sheer forces of their more recent history, represent the focus of universal pity and humanitarianism. Their unutterable poverty, misery and at times loss of original self-identity, status and self-confidence are better passed over here, to be treated later in this book.

Moreover, whereas the peoples of European descent in their obvious hegemony over the rest of the world in the fields of science and technology automatically stand unequaled in their capacity to disseminate not only acquired scientific knowledge but also, and perhaps inevitably, their culture, their will and their ideals, the peoples of African descent, because of their involuntary exposure and because of what has become of their heritage, are about the most easily susceptible to these European influences. They hardly ever seem able to make their inner thoughts known, for various reasons: political and economic suppression, ignorance of relevant and crucial knowledge—the prerequisite of fair play—relative poverty of expression and lack of means of conveying expression.

The cardinal evil that emerges is a European monopoly which, however indeliberate or incidental, results in an incredible lack of rapport between the two groups. This engenders limitless scope for misunderstanding and indignation and forms a fertile ground for suspicion, bigotry and even hate. Peace in these circumstances is at best tenuous and tainted.

African political independence is the first essential step in correcting this potentially dangerous element in the relations between these two groups. It is to be hoped that as the African becomes more and more independent or self-sufficient, relations between him and the European will be more friendly, free of acrimony and mutually respectful.

The smaller and more closely interwoven world exerts a significant influence on patriotism and national conscience everywhere. There is an unmistakable trend toward a strict and earnest maintenance of national standards and morality and away from the double standard which allows harmful and irresponsible patriotism to be manifested abroad while constructive and responsible patriotism prevails at home. Indeed, modern patriotism is outward-looking rather than inward-looking; yet it is as vigorous as ever. Surely this is a blessed fertilizer to nourish and nuture universal human brotherhood.

This book was written at the close of a decade's sojourn in England: the first few years in London and the rest as an undergraduate, postgraduate and professional at Oxford. The same period was of utmost significance to all Africans, for it witnessed the uncompromising demand of all African peoples for the political right to shape and direct their own destiny, all by themselves. No literate African could have been uninterested in these events; all Africans were acutely conscious of the granite-hard fact that whatever might be their individual educational achievements in foreign lands, they were fully committed to return to the fatherland to share in whatever fate befell it.

To certain Africans the new age of political independence is remarkable, not because in their new self-consciousness and self-confidence they, in certain respects, look and feel uglier to themselves, but because some entertain the fear that Africa may well just be in a *remission* from foreign subordination. Others believe that Africa has already been swept irretrievably into Europe in the hurricane of Western civilization which followed hard on the heels of the Atlantic slave trade and colonialism, so that the African, increasingly and permanently, is a European in all respects except in external physical appearance, or that he is European except in the uncovered parts of his body. Humanity must undoubtedly be appalled by this African letdown. Nevertheless, this uglier African age remains one of unprecedented enlightenment, of new optimism and determinism. It can never again be the same. It cannot be nearly so bad again. Africa, for the first time in the last four centuries, can, at least for the moment, think, hear, see, feel, reason, judge and to some extent act for itself. Africa is now accessible and can interplay with all others. The real and true Africa has at last broken loose from its age-long schizophrenic existence.

The African, whatever his vocation, is in the middle of a drastic and dramatic revolution which makes itself felt even to the beggar and the invalid. Morally he is often to realize that in the middle of this turbulence, his education, for example, the possession of a university degree or a professional diploma, cannot be enough, nor can it constitute an end in itself but only a means—the means to develop, or even to discover, all his possible talents for the maximal benefit of national development rather than for the pursuit or fulfillment of some personal ambition. This is especially patent when his education has been financed from public funds.

Political consciousness and even self-awareness in every African, whatever his vocation, certainly mature as his contact with the outside world becomes more intimate and real. The more educated and informed the African, the greater his curiosity and interest in the factors responsible for the desperate socio-economic situation of his country; hence his willingness to contribute his little quota to rectification of the several complex problems that need urgent attention.

The truth is, all educated Africans are involved in the task of nation building; all are politically active and sensitive individuals, irrespective of whether they are civil servants, clergy, educationists, professionals, economists, industrialists, students, soldiers, writers, actors or career politicians. This should not be a surprising exposition. A considerable degree of political consciousness and a handsome armory of economic facts, figures and realities are highly necessary at international negotiations and meetings concerned with national development—a process that involves all aspects of national life. Without political and economic perspicacity these nation builders cannot competently assess, approve or reject the relevance and the stake of foreigners from all lands who are involved in the crusade of African development. Without political and economic comprehension, execution of plans and programs cannot be efficiently carried out, and carried out in the best and long-term interest of the African nation concerned.

Indeed, the struggle for human survival, for national or group survival, has shifted its center of gravity from the battlefield into conference halls and committee rooms; it involves less of bullets, bombs, muscle and brawn and more of brain power, nerves, foresight and crucial knowledge.

One of the crucial dilemmas that confront the African today is how to be (or aspire to be) himself in a genuine way without attracting undue attention from non-Africans and even from Africans; how to express himself without being flagrantly (or ostensibly) misunderstood and misjudged.

In international and interracial relations the amazing readiness with which an African is labeled a nationalist, a radical or an extremist, especially by non-Africans, often amounts, even if unwittingly, to a subtle denial of freedom of speech and expression. These labels immediately portray such an African as some irrational, aggressive and unfriendly misfit.

In the psychological warfare between the nations (a war which may only belong to the subconscious mind) terms such as nationalist, radical, extremist, terrorist, can often go a long way to castigate and vilify the personalities to whom they are relentlessly directed in the press, radio, TV and other mass media. The person who dares to step forward is often reflected to the rest of the world and to his own people as a nationalist, radical or extremist as if in fact he were an extremist, in the real sense, a man, pursuing so suicidal a course as might lead his people into ruin. Extremism in the true sense is absurdity, hotheadedness and recklessness which often may be difficult to dissociate from violence and even from psychological illness. The "moderates," on the other hand, are often paraded and played up as more reasonable and rational persons who represent the average and informed opinion of their people. The picture is painted that these African moderates represent the opinion of all rational and good people everywhere in the world.

If a radical is a man who advocates change not merely for the sake and the thrill of change but more for the sake of progress, prosperity, security, fair play and an improved standard of living, then without radicals the whole world would be static, decadent or dead. To an appreciable degree everyone is a radical, and radicalism is a universal trait. It is the sum total of brilliance, conviction, honesty, dedication, enterprise and progressiveness. The antitheses of radicalism are lethargy, indifference, irresponsibility, complacency and laziness, all of which constitute real danger to survival. The early Christian missionaries were radicals in so far as they carried the gospels across the oceans to distant lands, in much the same way as are the capitalists, the communists, the educationists and the humanitarians of our own time. The scientist who performs experiments which can bring about fundamental changes is a radical. Those who resist change and those who would rather stay at home to conserve and preserve their cultural heritage and ancestral shibboleths are also radicals in so far as they offer resistance to the normal course. All those who would endeavor to keep up with the tempo of the modern world—administrators, statesmen, churchmen, teachers, fashion designers, entertainers—are also radicals.

If a nationalist is a man who has a sensible perspective of the problems of his country and advances the legitimate aspirations of his people, it means that politicians and statesmen in all lands are nationalists and the African nationalist is not an extraordinary departure from the norm. Nationalism is a precondition for, if not synonymous with, patriotism and must therefore be regarded in general as an honorable feeling.

In fact and in practice the so-called African nationalists often belong to an educated African elite. African nationalists often prove in the long run to be the relatively better-informed and more farsighted Africans. They are the more genuine and more friendly types of Africans to non-Africans. African nationalists do not as a rule loathe non-Africans. Realistic and well-informed as they often are, they usually are the first among their own people to recognize the greatness in others and to appreciate other peoples' histories and culture. They simply do not want to be subservient to anyone, however great, noble or attractive.

They yearn for peace and fair play and abhor violence and domination. These so-called nationalists are often the Africans who are more likely to understand the forces of history and the true human values (in a contemporary and universal sense). They are the Africans who are more likely to assess accurately the real intentions and reactions of foreigners in any given instance. African nationalists are politically conscious and as such are acutely aware of their rights. They are reasonable, responsible and rational people who compare favorably in many ways with averagely informed and politically conscious citizens, politicians and statesmen in other parts of the world. Indeed, there is nothing particularly unique about the so-called African nationalists. They believe in themselves. They believe they were great and are potentially great, and can remain great in their own way. They also believe that all peoples are potentially equal and that the performances of any group or of any nation are largely preconditioned by the fortunes implicit in their environment.

The African moderate is that African who, through his ignorance or indifference, can often be counted upon at home and abroad to toe certain "cautious" lines on issues of domestic and foreign policy which are not necessarily in the best permanent interests of his own people. Though no less patriotic or courageous, he would accommodate a lot of what the so-called nationalists would not tolerate, simply because he is unsure and does not comprehend all the issues at stake. He just does not know, nor has he any answer whatever to the problems being raised. The so-called moderate often lacks the essential knowledge and the political adroitness, by the more competent and mature standards, to tackle the issues of modern politics and very often he cannot defend his case at any international forum or table with sufficient facts, figures, logic and confidence.

There is nothing whatever to suggest that the so-called African moderate is less patriotic or more friendly than the so-called African nationalist. The essential difference between the two is to be found in the level of their political awareness in the universal, in the international, sense.

It is bad and unhelpful not to know, but it is worse and hopeless not to aspire to know. It is hypocritical and malicious to know and yet pretend not to know—to know and not to tell. To hide the truth as if nothing were amiss is real fraud. To connive, acquiesce or condone is of no real good to anyone. To collaborate with what one is sure must be unjust and unfair, especially against one's own kith and kin, is the worst crime of all, for which no grateful thanks or genuine respect comes from any quarter. The value of being admired, praised and acclaimed depends on who are doing so, why they are doing so, and for how long they will do so. Who are these people? Are they for today—tomorrow—the next century—the next millennium? True and worthy admiration is that which continues for all time, in all impartial people, everywhere.

CHAPTER TWO

Their Golden Landmarks

Unless he is genuinely conscious that he has a past, however glorious or inglorious, the African who has been in contact with Western civilization and who has caught a glimpse of the richness and depth of the cultures of the East must certainly feel a sense or disillusionment and disorientation. As he visits the capitals of Europe and Asia he sees monuments, museums and innumerable relics of the past—landmarks which vividly reflect the noble achievements of centuries gone by. Is there anything in his African environment to compare or contrast with these? The questions must harry him by day and haunt him by night: What were his ancestors doing when such high intellectual achievements and cultural endeavors were taking place in these areas? Was his own great-grandfather a warrior or a statesman, a farmer or a weaver? Did he smelt iron or work glass? Where did he live? How did he conduct his daily life? What language or languages could he speak? What sort of possessions had he? What did his progenitors achieve, and where are the relics in the fields of human endeavor and skill? Did they rise like others, elsewhere, and or did they never rise at all?

Tremendous efforts are being made in several centers throughout the world to unravel Africa's past. To the African this is certainly one of the greatest romances of the second half of the twentieth century, for it invigorates his inner concept of himself as a world citizen who must exist as independently of others as anyone else can of him. The African feels firmly reassured in himself that he is not just an upstart—that his ancestors, in their own way, were as great as any.

The evidences of man's history before Christ are often foggy to all but the few who are specialists. It is only they who can pronounce with any degree of certainty and conviction that civilizations flourished in Africa at least a million years before Christ and that the Mende people who lived in the Upper Niger around 50,000 B.C. did some farming. It will suffice for the layman to have abiding faith in those available written records which he can comprehend. Most of these are in chronicles bequeathed to this generation by certain Arab and European scholars who visited Africa during the Middle Ages.

The history of medieval Africa is neither a myth, a fable nor a joke. It is not a philanthropic or paternalistic intellectualism fabricated to humor Africans. Rather, it is an impartial consensus of hundreds of authentic documents and maps synthesized only within the last two decades by certain dedicated European and African scholars, to put into proper and unprejudiced perspective the glories of medieval Africa, which were obscured and scandalized amid the embarrassments of the slave trade in Africa. It is true that certain gaps in our knowledge still need to be filled and loose ends need tying up. Yet the scaffoldings, for practical purposes, are already available for the world to see in the libraries and museums of Addis Ababa, Dakar, Ibadan, Kaduna and Paris. Moreover, no contemporaneous document has ever been advanced to contradict or refute the existence of the empires and kingdoms of old Africa.

Recent discoveries of the Nok culture in Northern Nigeria and of the Zimbabwe culture have opened up new mines of information about Africa's past.

To the African of this generation the true knowledge of old Africa is of enormous value. It allows him an inner ring of self-defense. It is an irreplaceable feather in his cap, bestowing upon him the greatest self-confidence to meet some of the challenges created by his inevitable and constant contact with people from other continents. He is indeed reassured that Africa is re-emerging, and not just emerging for the first time.

Basil Davidson's *Old Africa Rediscovered* and *The African Past* are among the better-known works on this subject. Davidson, in *The African Past,* comments: "We are only at the beginning of a coherent study of the African Past, and consequently of the documents concerned with it. I have drawn on 113 authors of whom nearly a third are African, including some who are famous, and others who are not, but generally avoiding the very obscure or the very well-known . . . [as the latter] can be quickly found elsewhere."

The writings of such veteran travelers as Ibn Battuta (1304–77), Leo Africanus (A.D. 16), Al Bekri (1067) and Delafosse are now common knowledge to all who are interested in the golden age of Africa. All these documents have proved beyond any shadow of doubt that great empires and kingdoms flourished in all sections of Africa long before the European dreamt of the continent.

There is neither the space nor the intention here to deal in any detail with those empires and kingdoms which lasted until the end of the last century, when they were confronted and smashed by European conquest, at times after years of prolonged and remittent wars.

To the south was the Zulu empire; to the east were the kingdoms of Bunyoro and Buganda; in Central Africa were the Matabele and Mashona kingdoms and the Congo kingdom. These empires are still quite fresh in mind, and there are living evidences in their descendants who still echo in public life in these areas.

The medieval history of West Africa provides such irresistibly fascinating features as to require mentioning if only to allow an insight into the highly organized nature, the phenomenal pitch, of social and cultural excellence attained by the Africans of that era.

The empire of Ghana, founded about A.D. 300 by Sonike, is the best-known of the old empires of the Western Sudan. Al Bekri's record translated from Arabic gives a description of the court of the king of Ghana as he witnessed it:

The King of Ghana can put 200,000 warriors in the field, more than 40,000 armed with bows and arrows. . . . When he gives audience to his people, to listen to their complaints and set them

to rights, he sits in a pavilion around which stand 10 pages
holding shields and gold-mounted swords, and on the right there
are the sons of the princes of his empire, splendidly clad with
gold plaited into their hair. The Governor of the city is seated
on the ground; in front of the King and all round him are his
viziers in the same position. The gate of the Chamber is guarded
by dogs of an excellent breed, who never leave the King's seat;
they wear collars of gold and silk, ornamented with the same
metals. The beginning of the Royal audience is announced by
the beating of a kind of drum which they call *deba*, made of a
long piece of hollowed wood. The people gather when they hear
this sound. . . .

The Ghana empire stretched westward from present-day
Sudan to include parts of Northern Nigeria, Sierra-Leone and
Senegal. Ghana fell about A.D. 1240, when it was overrun by
Sundiata. Mali, Wolata, Susu and Mossi were other great
empires.

The greatest of the emperors of the Western Sudan was probably Mansa Kankan Musa of Mali. "In 1342, the renowned
Emperor of Mali, Mansa Kankan Musa, left his capital on the
Upper Niger for a pilgrimage to Mecca, taking with him five
hundred slaves each bearing a staff weighing five hundred
mitqals of gold, a mitqal being then about one eighth of an ounce.
His passage through Cairo long echoed in memory."

Timbuktu, Djenne and Gao were famous university centers
of medieval West Africa. Certain scholars from these universities were well known in Europe and in the Muslim world.
Ahmed Baba and Mahmud Kati were among the best-known.
"Here in Timbuktu," Leo Africanus wrote eighty years before
the Moroccan conquest, "there are great stores of doctors, judges,
priests and other learned men, bountifully maintained at the
King's cost and charges. And hither are brought diverse manu-
scripts or written books out of Barbary, which are sold for more
money than any other merchandise."

Other empires, such as the Ashanti, Benin, Dahomey and
Yoruba, symbolized high political and cultural organizations before the advent of the European to the west coast of Africa.

CHAPTER THREE

Euro-African Dialogue

The Slave Trade and Colonialism

Man essentially is always man. He always has been and always will be, irrespective of his ethnic group, his geographical location, his station in life or the socio-economic level of his environment.

Man would remain moral—he would be *nice*—but only just so far as it will not cost him too much. The moment it becomes unbearable for him, he begins to fall short of his usual standards, however high these may have been.

Man is invariably an opportunist, to a greater or lesser degree. Anyone will exploit whatever he reckons to be an opportunity, whenever it is "safe" to do so. The margin of safety is related in particular to his needs, his conscience, his religious ethics (if any), his legal obligations and his reputation and personal prestige in society.

Thus exploitation of man by man is a common, even a natural, phenomenon, the poor and the weak serving as obvious preys to the strong and the rich, who themselves are poor tempted predators. (Hence some wonder if it is simply God's doing that exploitation should take place, and if so, whose sin is it, God's or man's? Indeed, they ask, What is a sin, and what is not a sin?)

Whoever finds himself exposed or leaves himself exposed to exploitation, or puts himself in any weak position, and not only that but also perpetuates that position, truly deserves whatever treatment is meted out to him. He deserves little sympathy, especially when others know that his position is of his own doing and that he has had every opportunity to correct it.

Again, it is of supreme importance to know one's self, one's weaknesses and one's powers, and to consolidate these by never underestimating one's opposite number—either in presuming that he is exactly like one or in presuming him to be moral or reliable. The fears and ambitions of that opposite number are entirely his own reserve; his heart can neither be truly searched nor fully known. His behavior and reaction therefore can often become quite startling, for better or for worse. And to be able to assess his ulterior motive, one has to begin by trying to understand the forces motivating him. It is only in this wise that one can be capable of coping with him adequately.

Four hundred years have elapsed since the first Europeans set foot on African soil. The story began with European discovery of a mysterious continent which had been practically cut off from the rest of humanity except for an occasional trickle of Arabs from the north.

Over the centuries the world has shrunk unbelievably. Science and technology have made it possible for Europe and Africa to whisper to each other and to be in continuous contact. No one of African descent and no one of Euorpean descent can easily succeed in completely tearing himself away, even for one moment, from the hard facts of the very checkered history between these two peoples. Yet the two are equally aware that in order to remain buoyant, whether as nations or as continents, they need to maintain a dialogue which, ideally, must be mutually beneficial and free of acrimony. Indeed, Europe and Africa must be in love with each other, in true love, and not in enmity or in morbid fear or suspicion.

To the African the over-all picture has been a strange mixture of untold woe and humanitarianism, of callous exploitation and vicious repression, arm in arm with the salvation of the spirit from darkness and of the flesh from disease, pain and misery.

The African of this generation must not allow all the untold woes and sufferings of his ancestors to dominate his thinking and jeopardize his relations with Europeans. Such an attitude would be unrealistic, ignorant and rather misguided. But as man cannot truly rationalize without having recourse to what amounts to his past experience, African past experience with Europe has a logical place in assessment of the present and also in prefabricating the future, looking *centuries* ahead. The African must therefore be circumspect without being suspicious, though he has reason enough to be deeply suspicious of whatever emanates from outside his own continent.

The more informed the European, the more aware he is that the African has nearly every reason under the sun to be apprehensive about him and even to loathe him. He may even develop a guilt complex, especially when he comes across the African who he is sure is reasonably conscious not only of history but also of the present and probably of what the future seems to be pregnant with. He is aware that "his" own people tortured the African relentlessly for over three hundred years of the Atlantic slave trade, prolonged into the attenuated, milder and even spiced overlordship of colonialism and then followed by the post-colonial remission. But what guarantee has anyone that if the situation had been in reverse the African would have been any more lenient toward the European?

The European guilt complex toward the African, where it exists, ranges from sincere regrets and sympathies that manifest themselves in various guises to the other extreme in which the European regards the past merely as the stark facts of history and proudly holds the African in perpetual derision and contempt, musing that Africans would have continued to enslave themselves anyway, that Africans have come to acquire the fruits and blessings of Western civilization and have had to pay for these, even at the prohibitive prices set in Europe. But the last is untrue: Africa was thriving vigorously before the first European traders and seamen arrived on the coasts of the continent.

The first Europeans to come to Africa were explorers, merchants and seamen. The earliest Europeans to visit Africa were often quite impressed by the cities and wealth and people they saw along both the east and west coasts.

They went ashore to cities as fine as all but a few they could have known in Europe. They watched a flourishing maritime trade in gold and iron and ivory and tortoise shell, beads and copper and cotton cloth, slaves and porcelain; and saw that they had stumbled on a world of commerce even larger, and perhaps wealthier, than anything that Europe knew.

To these European sailors of the last years of the fifteenth century the coast of eastern Africa could have seemed no less civilised than their own coast of Portugal. In the matter of wealth and knowledge of a wider world, it must have seemed a great deal more civilised. They were repeatedly surprised by the ease and substance of the ports and towns which they saw and sheltered in and plundered. They found themselves repeatedly disregarded as strange and uncouth. "When we had been two or three days at this place," says the laconic log-book of da Gama's flagship, the Sao Gabriel, of an encounter at a port that was probably Quelimane (above the Zambesi river), "two senhorrces of the country came to see us. They were very haughty; and valued nothing which we gave them."[1]

At first legitimate trade was carried on peacefully between the European merchants and the inhabitants of the coasts of Africa. Medieval Africans at first never regarded with much seriousness these early Europeans, who only came, traded and went. They often restricted their activities to the coastal strips and spent as short a time as possible in face of the health hazards and also because they were at first content with whatever they could trade on the coasts. But they soon learned; they soon began to see and to appreciate the phenomenal wealth of the continent, evidenced by the gold and ivory that arrived ceaselessly from the hinterland.

These sailors and merchants, having acquired an insight into the strengths and weaknesses of the people and of their leaders,

---

[1] Basil Davidson, *Old Africa Rediscovered* (Victor Gollanz, 1959), p. 165.

steadily began to establish their strongholds in the areas with which they had familiarized themselves.

> They were better armed. They were trained to ruthlessness. They wanted more than a simple monopoly of trade, ruinous though that would be for the coastal cities: they wanted loot as well. African warfare, like Indian warfare, was designed to minimise casualties, not to maximise them [but] these invaders had no such care.[2]

It was Alonzo Gonzales, a Portuguese, who tipped off his fellow countrymen to Africans, swearing that slaves bought from African chiefs would be more suited to the conditions on the sugar and tobacco plantations of the New World, where European and Indian indentured servants, paupers, rebels, victims of kidnaping, convicts and slaves easily perished in the harsh climate.

By 1450 the first African slaves had landed in the New World. For the next three hundred years slaves estimated at about forty million, mostly the toughest young men available, were uprooted from their native land.

The sale, the branding with hot iron, the chaining, the whipping and flogging, the packing prone like sardines, of the "black cargoes" in the deadly ships across the "middle passages," have been vividly described in many books, depicted in many films and told in many tongues and in all lands. The unutterable mental suffering and the unthinkable physical agonies and dehumanization which these, the poorest victims of man's inhumanity ever contrived, endured are rather left to the imagination than described. Today, to anyone, anywhere, it is in itself a mental suffering to listen, read or recount. These indeed were the zenith of anything, however prolonged, however painful, however hopeless, however helpless and however fraught with sad and endless sequelae.

Yet it must be grossly unfair and unjustified to restrict any condemnation there may be to the successive generations of European merchants and seamen for these alleged crimes. Suc-

---

[2] *Ibid.,* pp. 168-170.

cessive generations of African chiefs and noblemen must always bear a substantial fraction of the blame.

Some of the Africans were by no means passive victims or mere observers of these conflicts. Indeed, the trade would have languished without their wholehearted cooperation. Supplying slaves for the European powers was both the profession and the recreation of many native kings. It would be a great error to suppose that the rulers of Dahomey and Ashanti, for example, or the Damel of Cayor, in Senegal, were any more high-principled than Charles II, John Hawkins, or Queen Elizabeth I.

The African monarchs continued to control the coastal areas and in most cases owned even the land on which European forts were built. On the Gold Coast almost every local chief possessed a "note" or "book," that is, a legal contract issued by the European power controlling the fort in his area; the contract acknowledged his title to the land and fixed a yearly rent. Chiefs fought for possession of these "notes" exactly as European powers fought for the Asiento.[3] Except in Portuguese Angola, the Africans remained independent of the foreigners encamped on their shores. When the Dutch, in 1637, tried to subjugate the local tribes around Elmina, they suffered a costly defeat. The chiefs were sometimes taken to Europe, where they were lavishly entertained and met the rulers. The king of Whydah acted as an arbiter in disputes between the European nations trading in his little dominion, and his decisions were accepted without question. The king of Dahomey seldom shook hands with a white man, and then only as "a very uncommon mark of royal condescension." A French trader complained in 1630, "The great wealth of the Fantineans (Fanti) makes them so proud and haughty that a European trading there must stand bare to them." A Dutch slaver reported that in Anamabo, the English factors dare not in the least contradict the local kings but are rather obliged to bear with them and are sometimes so invested that they are confined close to the castle without daring to stir abroad. Nay, if the Blacks dislike the English chief factor, they send him away in canoe to Cape Corso (Cape Coast Castle) or oblige him to pay a heavy fine. Salutes had to be fired in honour of the local king by every ship that put into port, and an English captain who

---

[3] Official license to deal in slaves.

omitted this courtesy on the Gambia was arrested by the king and heavily fined.[4]

The major effect of the slave trade on Africa was depopulation: the continent was robbed of its most able-bodied young men, who had the highest market value. No one could have matched impassioned Dr. W. E. B. Du Bois in summing up the story: ". . . whole regions were depopulated, whole tribes disappeared. It was the rape of a continent, seldom if ever paralleled in ancient or modern history." The Africa that had been highly organized had retreated into its clay age: totally fragmented, broken of will and of incentive. Popular occupations among the people no longer included legitimate trade, manufacturing, farming, creative art and handicraft; there was only the hide-and-seek of slave hunting, an effort which reportedly accounted for about 10 per cent of all the citizens being carried away. The economy was severely crippled, what with European guns, rum, brandy, beads, swords, etcetera, dumped generously on the coasts and in the hinterlands of the continent. Social life steadily ground to a standstill and eventually went into decay. So also cultural life. Political institutions were disintegrated. The strategy, thought and fright of wars haunted the tribes who fled into the jungles. Cities, villages, farms and markets were either deserted or razed in flames. For the greater part of the 350 years of the slave trade, the whole continent was in a state of perpetual siege, nervous, delirious and unpredictable; wars raged incessantly and with increasing expertise, thanks to imported guns and swords.

Racism, racial hatred or contempt for the African never primarily motivated the trade itself, but the trade needed some justification, if only to pacify a section of opinion in Europe. Various myths had to be evoked: that the African was not in fact a man but a subhuman being which deserved the treatment being meted out to it. The trade had become imperative, if not vital, to meet the desperate demands for cheap labor in the plantations of the New World.

---

[4] Mannix and Cowley, *The Black Cargoes* (Viking Press, 1962), p. 30.

The Portuguese enjoyed a monopoly of the trade for the first two decades. The British, French, Dutch, Spaniards, Germans and Americans soon joined. With increased international competition in Europe the trade came to be regarded as indispensable to any national economy.

The number of Africans shipped away into the New World grew with the years and the decades. The trade reached its peak in the middle of the eighteenth century, the century that welcomed seven million Africans on the coasts of America. The English, all alone, accounted for three million of these. This figure would exclude those who perished on the way through illness or epidemics or who were thrown overboard to lighten the ships or who committed suicide on their way into the unknown.

Throughout the incredibly long interval of three centuries that it occurred, an occasional voice became audible here and there in Europe and the Americas, protesting against this exceedingly lucrative European international enterprise. The trade was no longer the responsibility of young merchants and veterans like John Hawkins; it enlisted influential support from prominent personalities of church and state in various cities of Europe.

It was the Society of Friends (Quakers) who made the first determined and convincing effort toward abolition of the slave trade. In England, Sharp, Stephens, Clarkson, Wilberforce, Ramsay and Fox were among the foremost champions of the anti-slavery cause. A significant landmark was reached in 1772, when Lord Mansfield, in the case of a slave called Somerset, ruled that the state of slavery was not recognized by the law in England; henceforth any slave who was already in England or who could set foot there was a free citizen.

The most unfortunate aspect of the Atlantic slave trade was not the enslavement itself but the hopelessness and permanence of status that it was to engender. The slave identity typified by his dark skin in the New World could be obliterated merely by miscegenation, assimiliating the two most racially distinct groups into each other, to produce a stock that would be less prone to racial bigotry. In the north such miscegenation as took place was clandestine, and up until today (1967) state laws in thirteen states of the United States still forbid interracial marriages. In South America the situation was different: the Spanish, Portuguese, Africans and Indians all mixed their blood rather freely, and it often is claimed that racial discrimination and color prejudice are practically non-existent in these areas until this day.

Whereas any European who entered the New World before 1865 might well have been an indentured servant or a victim of kidnaping or a slave, by virtue of his race or color he could easily throw away his shackles and quickly climb up the existing social ladder. Not so the African. The presence of any African in the New World had one and only one explanation—the slave trade. Thus the unmistakable identity of the African as the accredited serf or subordinate of the European in the New World was born. *Negro* was a euphemism for *slave*: until qualified or proved otherwise, "that slave" meant "that Negro," and vice versa. Freedom was denied in every sense: freedom of movement, of association, of speech. Religion, education and public assembly were prohibited. Each slave soon learned to look up to his master as his only means of survival. The slaves were often docile to the extent that some slave owners could compare them to their domestic animals, which would neither abscond nor insurrect.

Over the course of three hundred years only 250 slave plots and revolts were reported, an amazingly low figure in view of the length of time and the millions of slaves involved. Some of the reported incidents probably amounted only to nervousness or suspicion on the part of the slaveowners. One such revolt gave birth to the Republic of Haiti in 1804. Certain other slaves occasionally responded with idleness, sabotage, and "praedial larceny," that is, the stealing of crops.

The human spirit can prove quite unsinkable indeed. These unfortunate Africans, suddenly hauled from their fatherland into the glaring and dazzling lights of European civilization, managed to retain a bit of theirs. The African awakened after the long nightmare of the middle passage to find himself without his blood, his water and his food, without his raiment, his lyric and his folklore; he had become destitute and shameless in the midst of all that meant endless shame. He was compelled to begin life all over again. Whatever remained of friends, families and colleagues had been fractionated and polarized to serve in different locations and homes in unknown and uncharted lands. Intuition called for adjustments: to make the best out of the worst lot. The way of life changed drastically. Languages, folklores and even names steadily faded out. Whatever aspects of African culture were imported steadily withered, to be eclipsed by European culture and sense of values.

The next step, after the stage had been set for a stable, prosperous and promising America, with African immigrants clearly established at the lowest stratum, was a mass exodus from Europe. In the two decades 1840–60, Ireland alone sent 3.3 million of her people (40 per cent of her population) into the New World, principally into the United States. About 1.28 million people emigrated from Europe into the United States alone in the years 1906–7; these came mainly from the poorer classes and the unemployed—the casualties of European industrialization and the population explosion which accompanied it.

Certain cardinal points must never be omitted in any objective study of the Atlantic slave trade, as they are pertinent to the sequelae of the slave trade which are still evident in various parts of the world and are relevant in interracial relations.

First, even before the advent of the European to the coast of Africa, slavery was a well-established institution. Slaves were usually war prisoners, and their descendants often automatically assumed the status of slave.

Slavery in Africa was an ancient and widespread institution, but it was especially prevalent in the Sudan. Mungo Park, after his journey to the Niger, estimated that three quarters of the inhabitants of the many Kingdoms through which he passed were slaves. It has been claimed that African slavery was a very different institution from slavery in the New World, as the owners were not driven by the desire to make large profits from their chattels. Gustavus-Vassa, the only slave shipped from Africa who acquired a sufficient mastery of English to write an account of his life, says, in recounting his boyhood memories, "Those prisoners (of war) not sold or redeemed were kept as slaves but how different was their condition from that of the slaves in the West Indies. With us they do no more work than other members of the community, even their masters food, clothing and lodging were nearly the same as theirs and there was scarcely any other difference between them than a superior degree of importance which the head of a family professes in our state. Mary Kingsley, the English missionary-anthropologist, defines African slavery as a state of servitude guarded by rights.[5]

Second, a good fraction of Africans shipped to the New World had never been slaves as such on African soil but had been captives in the intertribal or interethnic wars fought purposely in order to avoid ultimate enslavement by European slave merchants; each group had to launch a preemptive attack on the other so as to avoid being descended upon by another group, equally well armed with the firearms provided by European cataclysm. Added to this widespread turmoil, some of the people sold into slavery were men, women and children, victim of local kidnaping, who had been arbitrarily seized by their fellow countrymen or Europeans in the act of slave hunting. It did not matter who he was, chief or chattel, anyone who was unfortunate enough to be overpowered by these raiders would be swept into the unknown abyss.

Third, the universal tendency today is to stigmatize unhesitatingly with slavery only those people of African descent in the New World. But a few of the first European and Asiatic immigrants into the New World were also slaves. Indeed, from time immemorial slavery had been a universal practice, and even until the eighteenth century women were still on sale in the Smithfield Market of London (see the *Times*, July 19, 1797). As this was the case, one could hardly expect anything much better than what is today regarded as sordid and inhuman treatment by those European merchants and seamen toward their African captives, who were strikingly different from them.

---

[5] Mannix and Cowley, *op. cit.*, p. 43.

Behind the thick dark clouds of these dismal centuries a few slaves were able to shine. Anton Amo was a notable one. Born on the Guinea coast in 1700, Amo was shipped away to the New World and grew up to become a professor in two European universities by the middle of the century. He was able to speak five European languages, and he later became a counselor in the court of Berlin. Ignatius Sancho, Attobah Coguamo and Gustavus Vassa were among others who distinguished themselves in Europe. In England certain Africans, "noble savages," objects of amazement and curiosity, were given responsible posts in the courts of George I and George IV.

By 1700 there were fifteen hundred slaves of African descent in London. Some of the slaves were later returned to Africa. Some of these founded Sierra Leone in 1786; some others established in Liberia in 1822.

Although slavery was abolished in England in 1833, for the next fifty years illegal trade continued, though with diminished ferocity.

The slave trade had been so lucrative that legitimate trade in ivory, gold, pepper and woven cloth was largely abandoned, if not rendered impossible by the slave trade itself. Man hunting certainly struck certain African chiefs as an easier and less hazardous task, with quicker profits, than hunting elephants to collect ivory or employing laborers to till the soil.

Colonialism became well organized after the abolition of the slave trade, or should it be said, the slave trade was an envenomed exacerbation of European colonialism, which had begun in the earlier decades of the fifteenth century. By the middle of the eighteenth century various European-owned companies had been established in parts of Africa to promote legitimate trade.

Some of them that began as private enterprises soon came under direct supervision of the metropolitan government. The reasons for the imperialists' endeavor to establish their influence and authority often varied with the particular African region. They were principally inspired by economic, military, emigrative or philanthropic considerations; often they were due to missionary zeal, at other times to sheer patriotism and the ambition to dominate the world.

In 1482, Portugal overran and subdued Angola. For the next three hundred years other European powers followed the example of Portugal—annexing or seizing various regions, swindling, tricking, cajoling the chiefs and elders of the continent, many of whom were as greedy and unconscionable as they were hospitable and ignorant. By her attack on Ethiopia in 1935, Italy achieved, for Europe, the complete subjugation of all African peoples under the system of colonialism.

Indeed, the whole of Africa eventually became a colony of Europe. Colonialism was a conquest, and at the least is best regarded as such by all and sundry. It was certainly a diplomatic or a psychological victory by which the over-all destiny of the continent passed into the hands of groups of people who were completely foreign, and obviously different racially, culturally and socially.

The era of colonialism in Africa was characterized by a continental political stupor, each section sealed away, snoring in its own watertight compartment. There were often the sweet dreams of a better life, nightmares and night terrors of bloodshed and of physical, vocal and mental repression. There were the soothing lullabies of Christianity, with promises and hopefulness for a better life. There were the sleepwalks of hundreds and thousands to labor, at times forcibly, on the plantations and in the mines. There was the intoxication of a brand-new culture, the analgesia and panacea of European medicine. In the name of the Lord, and as a matter of law, "law and order" was maintained.

Throughout the decades of colonialism the mineral and agricultural resources of Africa were steadily ploughed away to Europe. Africans at various points of the continent formed the faithful battalions of laborers who toiled for foreigners from the other side of the world who had by then installed themselves as overlords in the land that was the Africans' birthright.

Absurd and unjust legal acts, untenable by democratic standards even in the metropolitan country concerned, were often in operation to compel the African to work.

Each colony became the dumping ground for the finished products of the imperial country. These products often sold at the very same prices as obtained in Europe.

There was a palpable element of indifference which bordered on irresponsibility in the operation of colonialism by an imperial government. This government never took the affairs, welfare, destiny and aspirations of the citizens of the colonies with much seriousness. This indifference was implicit, until there was an eruption which re-echoed in Europe to alarm and alert everyone to the injustices being perpetrated by their compatriots in these far-distant lands. The metropolitan government at best exerted only remote influence or authority on their citizens who were away in Africa searching for profits. The colonial enterprise was invariably free; it received every support, moral, political and financial, from private agencies and governments in Europe.

The African spirit was never completely subdued, even where indirect rule prevailed in its apparently innocent serenity. Power there was, but only a few Africans were quite conscious of whence it emanated. The system was eminently clever, efficient and effective; it ensured the maintenance of law and order and the undisturbed daily output of the African worker ants, with minimal deployment of soldiers, policemen and blood.

Rebellion and discontent occasionally soared to the boiling point. Grievances varied with the particular area. Taxation, low wages, shaky land tenure, forced labor, racial discrimination, denial of rights to form independent churches and to found schools—these often were enough to precipitate rebellions against the colonial regime which at various times resulted in bloodshed and loss of lives. In West Africa colonial insurrections occurred in Ashanti, in Benin and in the eastern provinces of Nigeria. By 1913, Lugard had completed the armed subordination of the northern provinces of Nigeria. Mass rebellions occurred sporadically. Thousands of lives were lost in each of the following well-documented rebellions: the Tanganyika rebellion of 1906, the Mashona-Matabele rebellion of Rhodesia, the Bantete rebellion of Natal, South Africa, and the Mau Mau rebellion of Kenya.

The population of the Belgian Congo is alleged to have been whittled by 7.5 million between 1900 and 1960.

Any social or welfare development that occurred under the aegis of the colonial government amounted to a capital investment calculated to step up production of raw materials and at the same time facilitate their convenient export from the African coasts into imperial Europe. All roads, railways, seaports and telecommunications were constructed with this fundamental aim in mind: they were not meant to promote social intercourse among the various components of the countries.

When the appetite of the home country had been satisfied, the rest of the raw material was sold to other European countries and America at colossal profits. Practically all the profits went into the development of the imperial country. By this system of trade Africa was continuously bled from various areas to transfuse and invigorate Europe and increase the general standard of living of its citizens.

Portugal administered her African possessions as integral parts of the mother country. The social system allowed an African to graduate into a European when he had assimilated enough of European culture.

The same principle guided the social element implicit in French colonialism: Africans were to develop the illusion that they were Frenchmen by a process of assimilation of French cultural values and were encouraged to cultivate French patriotism by holding responsible posts in an empire which had its heart and its soul in Paris.

The Belgian Congo was the personal property of King Leopold II from 1876 to 1908, when its ownership was transferred into the hands of the Belgian government after a commission of inquiry had exposed the heinous crimes that were being perpetrated in this region.

The British were rather less concerned with assimilating their colonial subjects into British culture. In no instance were the colonies represented in Parliament. Rather there was a colonial secretary who exerted his remote yet final control over the

colonial subjects who were governed by the British governor
resident in each colony.

Alongside the trading and administrative elements of the imperial influence were the Christian missionaries, doctors, nurses
and others whose sole purpose it was to add salt to the life of the
African bereaved, sickened and emasculated after the long
storms and ravages of the slave trade and its consequent social
and cultural degeneration, depopulation and disorganization of
established society. Wherever and whenever pain was inflicted
by their compatriots, these missionaries and humanitarians provided the cool, soothing and reassuring air to relieve such pains.
Indeed, they served Africa to the best of their ability in often
terrible and challenging circumstances. Nevertheless, the manifold challenge that confronted them was to resolve the various
bizarre conflicts posed by European national patriotism, Christianity and the certainty or conviction that the African was just
another human being and a potential candidate for the kingdom
of God.

It was through the gallant efforts and dedication of the Christian missionaries that the first schools in the Western pattern and
Western writing, language and culture made their effective penetration into Africa. These European Christians also undertook
civilian efforts.

> The missionary was an Admirable Crichton not because he
> combined a number of politico-economic functions useful to his
> native country, but because he had to adapt himself to different
> trades in order to build up his own mission on the spot. He was
> architect, builder, mason, road engineer and planter; it was in
> this kind of versatility that he had strong affinities with that other
> admirable Crichton, the Colonial officer in charge of a piece of
> "virgin territory."[6]

But the Christian missionary effort never attained much usefulness in certain areas of Africa. In the Congo, where education

---

[6] Robert Delavignette, *Christianity and Colonialism* (Burns & Oates,
1964), p. 66.

had been left in the hands of the Roman Catholics, on the eve of political independence, in 1960, only about a dozen Congolese citizens had attained university qualifications of any description.

The Christian's dilemma under colonialism was to be forced into acquiescence in many instances or get thrown out by his more worldly European compatriot; he had to content himself with dissemination of the Gospel and condone the painfully stark facts of colonial profiteering, exploitation and un-Christian legislations and attitudes of which to pretend ignorance would in fact be more sinful than mere condonation. But the salient and inescapable question is, What, after all, is the essence of Christianity? Be that as it may, the Christian could heave with relief: his aspiration must have been fulfilled on seeing some of his old students and the children he loved emerge in later years to challenge, all by themselves, the injustices of colonial economy and autocracy and to champion the cause of their national independence.

The imperial powers, having made their entry, forced or through heavily one-sided treaties or legal fictions, retreated very much into the background and left the limelight to chiefs and elders whom they easily maneuvered from behind the scene. The ordinary man in the street was often totally oblivious of the significance of the influence wielded by the European foreigner; to him the Europeans were innocuous friends and traders who were helping to build the country and bring about "progress"; and some were helping to foster the cause of peace, even among the elders, and to spread the Holy Gospel, which promised so very much. Everywhere on the continent the European was usually quite friendly and a whole town or village quickly fell under the spell of a single misionary who represented everything that was noble, innocent and humanitarian. This Christian stereotype was also reflected on other Europeans seen around. Those of them who never worshiped with Africans were assumed to have some other means of adequately fulfilling the demands of the Christian faith.

The European peace-loving outlook and progressive influence

(what with all the superior goods, efficient machines, gunfire, education, medicine and other novelties) were usually reassuring to any sane African king and his court.

It was the belief that the European had little or nothing to gain but a curious sense of adventure by coming from across the high seas, with all the risks involved, into Africa; it was a personal sacrifice inspired by the Christian faith.

It is inconceivable that even after the potentialities exhibited by the Europeans, some of the African leaders should have surrendered their destiny and their heritage so cheaply into the hands of the foreigners. It soon became apparently logical and right that the European should have bought and paid for a piece of land, then employed the indigenous population to work on that piece of land, with their housing and daily bread ensured. European capitalism preyed on crass African ignorance and also on the greed and myopia of African chiefs and landlords.

The first decisive disadvantage of colonialism to the African was the fact that the various imperial powers, having agreed among themselves back home in Europe, enjoyed complete monopoly in particular areas of Africa. In such circumstances the African automatically lost practically all his bargaining power.

With inscrutable impartiality, the influence of the European became increasingly powerful. Soon he was able to attain the implicit confidence of all and sundry in any local dispute. He occasionally sponsored rival candidates for vacant thrones and other political posts. He often supported tottering and insecure regimes with his personal influence and, when necessary, with threats and armed intervention. In the end, real power and all discretion became his. With the police and the army fully established, all the levers of power were securely in the hands of the colonial administrator. African chiefs, elders and noblemen soon got to appreciate this fact and adapted themselves accordingly. They gradually declined in their influence and authority. The educated elite, or middle class, on the other hand, acquired more personal freedom, beyond the control of the chiefs.

Through the efficient system of indirect rule, it soon became possible for a young European administrator, in his early twenties, to have wide expanses of African land and populations often running into the millions completely under his thumb, while the armed forces paid public homage to him and extolled him in spite of the chiefs and elders, who had become puppets.

The ordinary man merely felt the radiancy of power, and with this a new and relatively more lively environment. In his ignorance, until he was actually evicted from his piece of land, he was the absolute owner of that land. In a contest with his head chief, with a European referee he would win and retain his ownership. He never knew that in the international law that really mattered, the same piece of land had already been signed off, and belonged ultimately to some foreign imperial power represented by the young man he saw only once in a long while. To his mind he was getting the best bargain possible for his goods, for his sweat, not knowing that it was possible the very same goods as packed out of his land could bring him manifold profit and even transform his life and his energies and save him unlimited sweat. He could not stop to imagine that his ignorance was being exploited by anyone.

The ordinary African was often either cordial or indifferent to the European presence in Africa. Most Africans were even unaware of the real purpose of the presence of the European, whose visits were few and far between; his purpose was exerted through several intermediaries. He usually kept his distance, often living remotely on the hills or in some cosy environment which had been a virgin land, far removed from residential areas. He might take one or two African servants with him, but he seldom slept under the same roof with them. No one knew and no one bothered much about his way of life; he was never shadowed; he was simply seen moving here and there; his comings and goings were of no interest to anyone, and no one was interested in knowing to whom he was actually responsible. He was usually quite confident, appeared rich and prosperous, independent of action and of will, never seeking the advice or the favors of any local African on any issue; he was rather paternalistic, giving away presents and inviting chiefs and elders on rare occasions to tea or such little social functions, without honoring anyone's personal invitation in return.

European colonialism in Africa was in two rather different forms. First, in areas to the north and west of the Congo River, where the environment proved unsuitable for European settlement, only few could brave the insalubrious conditions provided by the harsh tropical climate and virulent diseases and settle down permanently.

Second, in areas, especially to the east and in Southern Africa, where the climate was rather more favorable and economic attraction (provided by the discovery of gold in Witwatersrand in 1854, and of diamonds in 1870) proved irresistible and promising, emigrants from Europe came by the thousands to make their homes and to commit themselves to Africa. World War I was also responsible for a large influx of Europeans into Africa.

It was in the eastern and southern parts of the continent that European hegemony was exerted to its very maximum and manifested itself in every facet of the social, political and economic life of the indigenous population. In these areas European immigrants either operated as individual farmers or belonged to European trading, mining or farming monopolies. Whereas the indigenous African can be said to have been self-sufficient—being able, within the context of his tribe, to grow his own crops, weave his own cloth, till his soil, rear his livestock, fetch his water, build his huts and take active and responsible part in the village life of his ancestors and on the whole make all ends meet without neglecting the trust of his family or the clan—it was the colonial government's introduction of taxes, payable only in cash, that spelled his real doom and totally disorganized the established village life. The payment of tax in cash led to the replacement of a subsistence economy with a cash-money economy.

Although taxation was, at least ostensibly, to provide social amenities and improve the welfare of all and sundry, it nevertheless had the inescapable effect of compelling the African to go out of his way to find something new, rare and imported from

Europe. It was the introduction of this maddening and compulsive search for cash as a means of exchange and as a means of survival that constituted the *fons et origo* of all the evils that were to haunt and harry the African in his own fatherland. He had to sell his land and his energy; he had to compromise his family life and village life in his sleepless search for cash (European reimported copper, silver and gold) to pay the poll tax and the hut tax, and to buy the basic human needs—food, clothing, furniture, etcetera—which his untiring quests for cash would no longer allow him to get for himself. The Europeans had all the levers in their hands—the cash itself and the political power to enact laws and acts for the maintenance of peace and the promotion of more cash for all.

European money became the indispensable commodity, and the quest for this money became a curse on the African. With the wave of a hand large numbers of African families were forced out of competition; henceforth they were to be sent careering into European-owned plantations and mines as their only means of scratching an existence from the soil of Africa.

For one thing, the indigenous African could never match the European immigrant armed with capital, knowledge and experience acquired by virtue of having belonged to a wider and more robust world. European trading monopolies proved the most formidable of all—universal and overwhelming in strength, resourcefulness and trained personnel, they seemed never to have anything whatever to lose. The African was easily bought out of his own land, and before he knew where he was, over half of the best lands had passed into possession of these invading immigrants by processes whose sanctity and legality were consecrated with spurious and dramatic formalities and reassuring ceremonies.

Ultimately, with their first-rate knowledge of the continent of Africa and its mineral potentialities and agricultural possibilities, the European immigrants steadily bought, acquired or seized all the most fertile and mineral-rich areas of the continent from the indigenous farmers by paying at best only nominally for them.

The phenomenal profits made in Africa by European colonial-

ism can never again be equaled in the history of capitalism and
of the world: land was cheap, capital was easily and enthusiastically available from Europe, labor was as cheap as slave labor
in the New World and was at best only nominally paid for and
ensured or enforced by governmental legislation; raw materials
were available in fantastic quantities and obtained cheaply with
African sweat and toil, and there was no competition on the spot
from enterpreneurs of other nationalities.

The picture that emerged from this was that of the poor,
hungry and diseased African who had to live as the chattel of
the European on African soil. The European, the erstwhile immigrant, emerged as a comfortable, secure settler, with the posture
of the gracious benefactor out to feed, clothe and curse the
African. The picture of the impoverished African, the erstwhile content, self-sufficient indigene, a potential millionaire,
was sadly hidden; the rest of the world was simply presented
with the miserable element, who was to be advertised outside his
continent as a poor, barbarous, ignorant, voteless illiterate, without bothering to qualify how he came to meet this fate.

Heaped upon all this were the fabrications and legal fictions
calculated to aggravate and perpetuate the African's condition as
the dregs of the new society, to dehumanize him to the extent
that his will power would melt under the African sun: he was
to leave his family and walk miles to seek employment, which
often was available only on short contracts. This nomadic African
laborer received the barest minimum wage; he never acquired
any particular skill. In the worst-hit areas the African was never
allowed any form of association to advance his rights as a laborer
or as a citizen. By virtue of his temporary status his employer
would not bother about health facilities, holidays, housing, insurance, old-age pensions and other social amenities and elements
of personal security, some of which were already well known to
workers in Europe. Intergovermental agreements were in operation for the recruitment of specified numbers of laborers annually.
African chiefs and other indigenes often proved themselves, as
during the era of the Atlantic slave trade, ready middlemen in
this callous and stupid enterprise.

The hundreds of obnoxious repressive and oppressive measures which were in use in parts of Africa to keep those of European descent in perpetual hegemony have been vividly described in various books. Suffice it to say that it was in these countries that justice itself came into open conflict with the maintenance of the peace and contradicted what were paraded as laws; terror pervaded the atmosphere, placing an endless curfew on the peace; the individual, African or European, became so intoxicated with the blood in his veins and so overburdened by the color he wore that he became a helpless and hopeless victim of transient wishes and regrets about his own identity. He was so obsessively conscious of the armamentarium he needed or already had that he often was in danger of waging war with himself. In short, justice, peace, law, terrorism, happiness and security, each in its own way, became exceedingly subjective and carried little of its usual meaning, or even contradicted itself.

In certain parts of Africa, and especially in areas with heavy distribution of settlers, familiarity with the African was regarded as breeding contempt for the European population. In 1832 an editorial in Southern Rhodesia warned visitors from Europe—

In the name of science certain Englishmen enter this country to make exhaustive studies of the customs and habits of African tribes and in the process they conduct themselves in such a way that they lose the deference traditionally accorded to white men by Africans. At one time, Africans treated all Europeans with a certain deference; later they contrived to distinguish between those Europeans who were worthy of their deference by reason of their intelligence and character and those who were not.

Nowadays, those Europeans whose attitude to Africans has not only been correct, but benevolent, are losing this deference, and this is partly due to the antics of the so-called scientists.

These latter, who, from the very nature of their studies are usually advanced politicians, like to live as closely to the African way of life as they can. They imagine that by living very much as the African lives, in his village, they will gain the African's confidence and discover the secrets of his personality.

Frankly we think that much of this anthropological or sociological study is "hooey." It is interesting and possibly useful to investigate a tribal structure and ascertain in what respects one tribe differs from another. It may be useful too to probe the etymology of an African language, but there are many minutiae of conduct and language which are not worth the time spent on them. The proper study of mankind may be man, but there is no need to labour this study unnecessarily, and it is not necessary to drop to the African level of village life in order to get Africans to talk and unburden themselves into the life they are examining. They think what they want to think. In the process of the investigation they show the Africans what they want to find and the Africans naturally provide. This European familiarity with African breeds contempt. European men have lived with African women without losing much deference from Africans, but there are Europeans, who do not live with African women, but who live according to African standards, who therefore lose that deference. When Africans see European scientific men, who are considered by them to be a better type of European, behaving as if they were Africans, then they lose their deference and respect for all Europeans. This is not fair to the decent, kindly settlers of Northern Rhodesia who have won this deference by their careful mode of life.

Moreover, such sociologists can disturb the political atmosphere of the country. They can give Africans "wrong ideas." They treat them as if they were a grown-up responsible community when they are not, and they teach them to hate and resent the Europeans in the country whom they represent as exploiters. They may not be complete Communists, but they are uncommonly near being so.

This is not good enough. Why should the Europeans of this country tolerate these so-called sociologists who in the name of scientific research are injecting poison into our Race Relations? We settlers do not keep our wits about us half enough. We never seem to know what is going on at the other end of the country.

We do not ask sociologists to be Tories. They can be Communists if they like but they should behave like responsible Europeans during their investigations and they should not sow the seed of social and political discord.

If they attempt to do this they should be thrown out on their ear without any ceremony. We cannot afford to have such people in the country at the present time.

In areas with neglible European population, as in West Africa, racial discrimination was never officially enforced to the extent of provoking the indigenous population. The social situation was such that the African seldom needed or requested admission into clubs, hotels and other establishments owned by Europeans.

In Central and Southern Africa racial discrimination was the rule. The extreme, of course, is in South Africa and Southern Rhodesia, where Africans are confined into locations, townships and reserves and denied opportunities to improve their lot or compete, where it is possible, with European immigrants.

Some Africans grew to develop deep and genuine respect for the European, partly because he appeared a prosperous and knowledgeable foreigner and partly because the local chiefs and elders often trembled before his face. Superstitious as they often can be, especially when illiterate, some Africans believed that the European possessed fantastic magical powers (what with all his fantastic possessions—the large oceangoing ships, the airplane, the machine gun—and the secluded and serious life he lived) and that he could even become inanimate, invisible and attend private meetings, which in fact no doubt meant that someone had been leaking proceedings.

As would be expected, colonial education in schools and churches took, so far as possible, the pattern in the metropolitan country. Teachers and teacher trainers taught what they knew and naturally sought to promote the best interests of their native land, always seeking to attribute to it the best of everything. All attention had to be focused on the metropolitan country. Other countries, other political ideologies, cultures and religions, were insulated, winnowed out or proscribed by law. The European teachers had or showed no knowledge of medieval Africa: this would be irrelevant and even contradictory in a system that demanded a schoolchild to learn by heart and sing the patriotic songs of imperial countries, in European languages. African parents had little choice: their children must not be left behind in the inevitable new era; they must adopt Christianity, go to school, learn special foreign languages and strive to achieve those positions, in the civil service and in the church of Christ, usually reserved for the European under this system.

Because of the ghostlike presence of the European and the apparent legality and logic in whatever lands and enterprises he came to possess, it was not until after the First World War and under the inspiration of the Pan-African movement that the peoples of Africa began to be aware of the real meaning of the European presence in their lands. African students who studied in some of the great cities of Europe and America saw the light! They gained an insight into the European system of government and grew to appreciate the high standard of social justice— democracy, liberty, freedom of speech and association, funda- mental human rights—that they found in parts of Europe and North America. They saw the structure of the League of Nations and read deeply into the history of Euro-African relationships. They heard of the demands by Asiatic countries for self-govern- ment. Most importantly, they came into close contact with the European, lived and dined with him, in college and in public places. They saw the European in his homeland, as his ordinary self, outside the heaven he had created for himself in Africa. They often were challenged by the robustness of the European environment, by the wealth of European culture, by European history and by the European standard of living. Then, casting their mind's eye across oceans and lands, these African students in Europe and North America could see before them only the wilderness, the abject misery, the physical pain and the untold hardship in which their own people were living. Here indeed was the turning point! The challenge, the rage, the ambition and the sense of mission soon shifted their center of gravity to Africa. The untraveled, uninitiated Africans, still comatose from the emasculation and defacement of previous centuries, were to be aroused by the African elite into a new consciousness, by heart-rendering speeches, political meetings and demonstrations which groaned, wailed and demanded that various wrongs be put right. They were wrongs and injustices in so far as they did not obtain in the *mother country*. The educated Africans never failed to point out to the European administrator those things not done "at home" that he was seizing the opportunity provided by the African environment to practice in Africa. Steadily the veil was lifted. These post-slave-trade-era Africans began to gather in nooks and corners to hear what to them amounted to revelations—of the political, economic and cultural facts of European penetration and domination, and in certain areas, of attempts to obliterate the African ego. What was more, they were really convinced for the first time, in their own generation, that the European was in fact more *natural* than they had imagined him to be. These Africans then began to move closer and to study the European. They soon discovered that he possessed, at least to an appreciable degree, the same fears, sensitivities and passions, the same likes, dislikes and habits, they themselves knew and felt.

Thus the truth was born, afresh, and to a new generation of Africans—a generation that had been congenitally brainwashed, dazed or doped by the ignorance and myopia of their own forebears.

Of all the effects of colonialism, what disillusioned the African most was his feeling that he had been thoroughly cajoled and fooled; that he had indeed overestimated the European he saw and in whom he had reposed so much confidence. These exaggerated notions were suddenly and easily dispelled by the new African elite. But for this deep disillusionment, colonial revolt would probably have been less popular and spontaneous and the post-independence relations much closer.

The European, on the other hand, was confident and grossly underestimated the intelligence and capabilities of the African. While the European paternalized or disregarded the African, the African genuinely respected the European. This cannot be very surprising; the European could not have felt otherwise: there was very little by way of social intercourse between him and the African. Despite decades he saw very little of the caliber of the African. The European could only perceive the African in a subservient role—either domestically as his steward or chauffeur or professionally as his junior in the civil service, in the commercial house, on the plantations or in the mines. He could never gain a true insight into the African's real essence of life, his ideals, his standards, his morals and indeed his latent aspirations. The African, for his own part, had to struggle hard to attain and maintain his daily bread and cater for his dependents. It was therefore often difficult for him to show his real self to his European master. He had to cringe and maintain the fiction of his servant role. Nevertheless, it is a relieving thought that with the independent African taking his rightful seat in the comity of nations, he is able to show more of his potentialities. The former colonial civil servant looks across the hall in New York and Geneva to see so much good emerge out of Nazareth!

The slave trade had preceded colonialism and it had been fanned, at least partly and at least indirectly, by the European. Colonialism finally put an end to the inevitable intertribal wars of the slave-trade era. It also put an end to the institution of slavery within Africa and laid the basis for fundamental human rights among the people of Africa themselves.

The Berlin Conference dissection of the continent is 1885, followed by the defeat of Germany in World War I, has remained the basis for separating the peoples of different areas of the continent who are related only through contiguity, colonial tutelage and constitution rather than through cultural or ethnic ties. There are about forty such states, very weak states. One often wonders whether it would not have been a practical proposition for the conveners of the Berlin Conference, all members of the North Atlantic Treaty Organization, to reassemble, as soon as the discovery was made that the African was in actual fact capable of self-government and that he had even been governing himself before the advent of the European, and make efforts to create blocs that would be more hopefully viable and self-governing. Would the neglect to do this mean that the imperial powers had seen far ahead and calculated that it would be best to leave the business of African unity to Africans themselves?

Colonialism and Christianity both brought with them Western civilization, Western values, Western education and all the prerequisites that would make for a state in the generally accepted modern sense. The civil service, organized political parties, a democratic form of government and a knowledge of the world and of science and technology are among the other creditable things introduced into Africa through European colonialization of the continent.

The language of the imperial power became the lingua franca of each of the African countries administered, cementing the various ethnic or racial groups.

The various African countries had been borne, bred and baptized by the imperial mother country. After independence some changed their names, yet they have more or less retained their colonial structural identities. Could these various countries have been born otherwise? Africans must stop and ponder. Could they, now citizens of various nations, have achieved their present nationhood without colonialism? Could they have advanced even further and attained their industrial age without European colonialism? Could they possibly have developed entirely on their own, or through purely humanitarian or even altruistic European endeavors, or with the fraternal guidance of Africans who had gone to the New World if these had returned to the continent voluntarily, patriotically and in large numbers, and especially if their lot had been a bit better than it proved to be? There was Marcus Aurelius Garvey, the Jamaican who founded the Universal Negro Improvement Association in New York with the slogan "Back to Africa." A leader of this caliber might well have brought about the miracle of African political and economic independence. Garvey advocated that all Africans from the Americas and the West Indies be repatriated into Africa while the colonial powers withdrew. Garvey advocated a united Africa under one government, and once declared, "I know no natural boundary where the Negro is concerned. The whole world is my province until Africa is free."

Could a single force have unleashed itself within the continent and subdued as much of the continent as it could? Could the continent have been overrun by some other powers, Arab or Asiatic? Or could Africa, left completely alone in its schizophrenic exist-

ence, have evolved another type of civilization, even entirely
different from Western civilization and perhaps devoid of the
wheel and the machine; and the peoples of Africa remained
happy, content and comfortable, in good health and going about
their daily lives without being directly subservient to any
foreigners? Could Africans, through their own intuition, have
sailed to Europe and brought back Western civilization, or
crossed peacefully or through wars or in large pilgrimages to the
East and picked up new ideas to stimulate their native environment?

Be that as it may, Western civilization has made its deep
penetrations into the heart of Africa, and the pertinent question
now is, How should Africa react to it?

African reaction can be assessed in political, economic and
cultural terms. Emphasis will be laid in this chapter on the
political significance of the Euro-African dialogue. Since politics
and economics are always inextricably intertwined, the study
here will attempt to deal with the two subjects simultaneously.

First, what is the keynote of the dialogue between the peoples
of Africa and Europe? In her experience with Europe and with
the rest of the European world in the last four centuries, what
in fact has Africa learned? What has Africa gained? What has
Africa lost? What does slavery mean? When and how can we, or
do we, draw the lines between coerced, or forced, labor and
slavery; between capitalism and slavery? Has slavery, or even
the slave trade itself, stopped, or has it merely assumed a
modernized form, groomed to meet the conditions, disciplines,
conscience and circumstances of this age? Or perhaps the question makes more sense when asked in the negative. Africa has
always, since the inception of the Euro-African dialogue four
centuries, ago, groaned and fought for freedom from European
political and economic domination: Is Africa or a part thereof
really free? Even after political independence has been granted
and membership in the United Nations obtained, what can
African freedom mean to Africans, and what can it mean to non-
Africans? Can African freedom or the freedom of any bloc or
section of Africa ever become as full and as real as Chinese,

American or Swedish freedom or the freedom and independence of the empire of Mali or of Bunyoro?

Second, what are the real purposes of political independence, and how can these be achieved in the modern world? In view of the experience of the peoples of Africa in the last four centuries and their present pattern of development, can it be said that the African, already and forever, has lost the *will* and the *accountrements* for purposeful, self-respecting and progressive independence, the independence that will ensure a vigorous African continuity?

Third, the crucial questions of our age are: Does it matter, or does it make any difference, that the people who own, direct and control an enterprise in any country belong to a racially, religiously, ethnically, geographically, sexually or otherwise different group from those who are employed? When a man is employed by another, even by his own brother, has he not in fact been driven by a definite set of circumstances to seek this employment, or forced by a combination of circumstances to remain in this employment? When does employment amount to blackmail?

Not all men are created equal, in so far as some are deformed from the womb physically or mentally; they may have inherited adverse genes from their parents. But all normal men are potentially equal; yet they still are unequal and different in many ways, obvious or subtle, each man being a resultant of an equilibrium of diverse intrinsic and extrinsic forces which render him firm enough physically and mentally to appear an equal with others before the law and to deserve stipulated punishment for his crimes or praise for his valor. It is thus a cardinal tragedy that any two people, so long as they remain equal before the law, should be treated unequally, socio-economically or otherwise.

All normal men are potentially equal; those who work for a long period of time under any other must have been underprivileged at one stage or another in their lives. Setting aside such elements as luck and predestination, their deprivation may have been due to an inadequate social background or a lack of creative opportunities or such factors as poor education or lack of relevant and essential knowledge in the given locality; or it may have been related to conquest—armed, economic or psychological.

As regards nations, even when they are obviously unequal, each one still tries hard to be independent, especially of foreign nations which have no real stake in its own survival; the two cannot be equally exposed to the same threats. The tendency for nations to be free from foreign subordination is an irrepressible phenomenon so long as no two nations are equally exposed to the same threats—threats directed not only at physical survival but also at their respective economic, social, cultural or religious survivals.

A number of African countries are said to be free, but how much freedom do they really have or how much freedom can they ever have? Will the Nigeria of 2060 be any freer of the great powers of the time than the Nigeria of our age? Can Africa ever do without Europe, and can Europe ever do without Africa? There is no evidence to support the view that national or continental interdependence is a prerequisite for "development" or for the attainment of the popularly accepted civilized standard of living. If anything, interdependence spells national or continental insecurity, rather than self-sufficiency or the sincere desire for a universal human fellowship. Moreover, interdependence is not the same as peaceful coexistence; Africa before the fifteenth century was coexisting vigorously with Europe, albeit unespied. European intrusion into Africa upset this state of affairs, resulting in an uncalled-for dependence and the ardent demands for independence that ensued.

In the twentieth century, national or continental security has changed in meaning. All peoples the world over are almost equally affected by the possibility of sudden extinction. It is therefore only right that every country should be interested in the world outside its own frontiers; that everyone should be interested in the pursuit of peace throughout the world.

It is all too obvious that at the birth of the new African states, some of these states, if not stillborn, showed every sign of early death, and unless they were promptly resuscitated and invigorated by outside powers (usually, and perhaps morally, the mother countries that were responsible for the conception and contrivance of such congenitally handicapped states), they were doomed to perish or lose their sovereignty.

Some African states are so heavily dependent on outside help that if this help were withdrawn, the state apparatus would collapse instantly, with even more terrible poverty and hopelessness.

Today Africa (excluding South Africa, controlled by a minority of European settlers) is just as incredibly weak, practically defenseless and almost in the same sort of disarray as she was four centuries ago when the earliest Europeans arrived and with a handful of men with firearms (or with diplomacy) were able to sweep across the whole continent and keep the people in subjection and even in bondage. African internal communications are relatively still so poor that some of the countries are in practice nearer to Europe than they are to their nearest African neighbors.

It is safe to conclude, therefore, that the European departure from Africa, the surrender of political power into African hands, has been a sum total of imperial change of heart. This came about, not because Africa has proved a more hazardous military power to subdue or a stronger agitative force to contain, suppress or even smother, but mainly because of disagreement among the imperial powers in Europe, because of the jealous eyes and ideological warfare with the Communist world, and most importantly, the non-cooperation of the United States and her ambition to make her weight and influence felt throughout the world. Furthermore, in the metropolitan country, the conscience of the common man was awakened by various pressure groups—groups dedicated to carrying forth the home-cherished individual freedom and fundamental human rights to all lands. The League of Nations, and then the United Nations, exerted an influence and provided a new beacon of hope to all peoples who regarded themselves, or who were regarded by certain others, as being under some form of bondage. Nevertheless, the initiative rested

almost entirely on the imperial power concerned to voluntarily
surrender power. She retained this initiative and defiantly
asserted that it was her divine, internal and private concern,
rather than that of common humanity, religious ethics or natural
justice, to release her clutches on these countries only in her own
good time.

Whereas Europeans had always met among themselves to
deliberate about Africa, Africans have in their four centuries'
dialogue with Europe shown only a negligible amount of concerted initiative. This was difficult before the European penetration and was even more difficult afterward because of the turmoil
engendered by the slave trade and the watertight system enforced by colonialism.

This lack of collective initiative and cohesion kept Africa
disunited and permanently on the defensive in this dialogue.
Africa always had to wait for something to give in Europe before
starting to run helter-skelter in a crippling and helpless panic.

The absence of any form of Pan-African movement on the
Africans' soil itself mean that Africans had no appreciable
defense or thrust—they were incoherent, and any effort to advance their demands was based only on morals.

No leader ever toured his own country or the continent, none
was known whose influence and wisdom could have been acknowledged outside his own tribe, who could have been said to
speak for all Africa, even if this meant only a substantial region
thereof. The man who perhaps came nearest this was Dr. Aggrey
of the Gold Coast. All others who might have been imbued with
the same sense of mission were usually magnetized into the
European missionary fold. Chiefs, headmen and priests throughout the continent lived in their respective domains content with
whatever little power they had and uneasy in the radiancy of
the European presence, which they often felt even more than
their own people did.

The era of the slave trade was one of crippling lethargy and
pathological fright, and so far as development was concerned,
a sheer waste of time. There was stagnation and retardation
which crippled adventure, enterprise and politics. And for

decades afterward, that is, throughout the era of colonialism, because of the repression and restrictiveness of colonialism itself, no one dared to step out of his own locality. As such no real leader ever emerged. The colonial governors and other administrators were often aware of these facts. They knew that their own knowledge (or records) of the territory over which they ruled surpassed anyone else's; they often taunted all who put themselves forward as the leaders of the people, quizzing them on facts and figures about the country and asking them if they had been to this place or that, and if they had not, how could they lead people who had never heard of them or whom they knew next to nothing about!

It was the African elite who returned from European and American universities and those traveled soldiers of World War I who eventually transformed this state of stupor into one of gradual awakefulness. They were the first leaders to emerge. They were the first to be recognized internally by all citizens throughout their respective countries. They were the first national leaders to be recognized externally by the imperial powers and by these powers' competitors and adversaries. They were the ones who could form an effective political party presenting a substantial front. They were the ones who could be wooed and who could be entrusted with any form of post-independence leadership and with the integrity of the colony in which the imperial power still had a lot of their investments, their nationals and other vestiges of their influence.

The Winking Remission

Today slavery is a state deplored by all mankind, yet pockets of slavery are still present here and there. Political systems which amount to slavery in everything but name, or perhaps are worse than the Atlantic slave trade, are found in Southern Africa.

Whereas in the amorphous, clandestine world of the fifteenth to the nineteenth century it was impossible to bring any country that committed certain crimes to task, today the situation is strikingly different. There is a new powerful, inhibitive and restraining element: world opinion—the bastion of justice and freedom everywhere. No country, however incorrigible and thick-skinned, would completely turn a deaf ear to the opinion of the rest of the world and of humanity. World opinion is an invisible yet incredibly influential establishment. It is likely to wax from strength to strength as the world shrinks further and international relations become inexorably closer. World opinion condemns colonialism. It condemns imperialism and all forms of domination of one people by another in the fashion that engenders suppression and endangers self-determination and human dignity. The opinion of all humanity is sharply against racial discrimination and racial victimization and other types of persecution.

Moreover, in this era, most fortunately, every nation strives hard to avoid being regarded as the aggressor in any international dispute; localized wars stand the chance of escalating into a universal conflagration which would incinerate a substantial fraction of mankind, leaving no victor to bask in the joys and splendor of victory.

Although the African continent is always open to armed attack by the peoples of other continents, the more likely challenge, and the inescapable one at that, is the battlefield that has already shifted its center of gravity into international conference halls and into business, educational, legal, religious, cultural and diplomatic circles in every corner of the world. This new type of warfare with other continents, especially with peoples of European descent, also involves intelligence and secret-service networks; it involves the ability to assess the strength, circumstances and sources of weakness of the opposite number and to predict or discover their intentions and to influence these intentions, whether they are already formed or not.

The world has grown, it has shrunk, it has learned, it has become more disciplined and restrained, yet the world, the whole world, is still as brave and adventurous and all-conquering as ever before; it is still as unscrupulous, wicked and selfish; it is still as potentially desperate as it was centuries ago. Yet the world still has a conscience, a heart of gold; it still is capable of goodness and humanity. It is still full of halfhearted, unsure or hypocritical protestations. It would, at will, evoke myths and with a brazen face rationalize myths to suit challenging circumstances.

Today, as it was centuries ago, and especially in the century of the Industrial Revolution in Europe, Africa's resources, raw materials and markets and in certain parts manpower are all still as necessary, if not vital, as ever before to the economic advancement of Europe. At the same time Africa still thrives only through the allowance, charitableness and benevolence of Europe and America, and through the humanitarian spirit of peaceful coexistence. African economic and material development, in the increasingly Procrustean pattern she has adopted, has come to depend substantially on continued European magnanimity and indeed on European generosity, self-denial, self-restraint and guidance.

But amidst all these, man basically has not changed and will not change.

What, then, can Africa do in this uneasy confrontation? What can Europe do? What can Europe and Africa do together? What can the rest of the world do for Europe and Africa? And indeed what can humanity do? Are Africa and Europe tied together first by a competitive desire to survive and only after this by a bond of common humanity?

Since January, 1961, the United Nations economic bulletins on Africa have continued to remark that the bulk of African trade is conducted with the former imperial powers in Europe. This in fact means that Western Europe continues to dominate the trade of most African countries.

The prices for most African raw materials have fallen in recent years, while Europe continues to demand ever higher prices for her manufactured goods. This relationship is oiled with foreign aid which pours into the continent in increasing amounts, yet with diminishing economic effect. Most of the African countries are actually not better off financially than they were before political independence was granted to them. Furthermore, we must recall that internecine wars were fought among the various

ethnic groups on the coast and in the hinterland of Africa over
the course of three centuries to avert local enslavement or
domination and that these resulted in mass enslavement into the
New World and the attendant endless sequelae. There was, at the
time, African myopia, greed and acquisitiveness, rising to the
bait of European manufactured goods, rum, guns. Are these in
fact not analogous to the internecine cold war of development
which is quite discernible in Africa today—the competition to be
good boys in European, American or Asiatic eyes which results
in foreign aid being awarded to the favorites and the select
among these African states that have mutually conflicting (and
in places antagonistic) development programs and foreign
policies?

In many African countries, foreigners continue to exercise
their subtle domination over important aspects of national
economic and social development. Items such as newspapers,
radio, mercantile houses, industries, banks, insurance companies,
building corporations, defense, aviation and communication,
plantations and in some instances currency find the continued
help and the established influences of the erstwhile imperial
master indispensable. Usually the African countries themselves
voluntarily request these foreign aids, believing this to be the
only or perhaps the easiest or the surest way for their development. There may very well be little or no importance to attach
to these aspects of national development. Experts of all nations
may quote international laws and examples and expound that
this is the type of fashionable *interdependence* which exists even
with the prosperous nations of Europe in their relation with the
United States or the Soviet Union, but the question that con-
cerns each African country is a perfectly simple one: How can
she get the maximum wealth out of her own materials? Before
she gets her industrialization into full swing, how can she compete against manufactured goods from Europe, North America
and parts of Asia? How can she protect her new industries? How
can an African country speedily and truly develop toward
economic independence and avoid being overexploited in the
process—overexploited and outwitted to the extent that she is no

less dependent on foreign aid, foreign capital and foreign charity than she was a decade or two ago? Is exploitation by foreign powers a sine qua non of economic development in the poorer countries? Can the far-advanced countries not refrain from exploitation in their commendable earnest and moral desire to help the developing countries? What are the arguments for and against foreign monopolies and nationalization of foreign monopolies?

Whatever may be said, whatever the historian or the economist may say or whatever international laws anyone may quote, it suffices the ordinary African to note that his own country does not possess a single foreign monopoly anywhere, and all evidences point rigidly against any different prospect.

The purpose of national development is to raise the standard of living of all citizens to a decent level and to consolidate national security in every sense. Although Africa has all the required potentials, at the moment each country is faced with two colossal problems: the one, that of amassing the capital essential for development; the other, that of getting trained indigenes to execute development plans, think for the nation at crucial international meetings, operate the civil service efficiently and handle the administrative and technical segments of the industries and other establishments with all competence. Foreign investments are being invited into the private sector of the industries and other enterprises, and the various countries request loans from and are awarded grants by the richer countries. Needless to say, this is a very nervous way to develop. How long these foreign monopolies will last, exactly how they will eventually withdraw and how much control any African government can actually exert on them are all questions which everyone shudders to speculate upon.

It is quite obvious that Africa's development is involving her more and more with the wealthier and more advanced countries. A relationship which is not unlike colonialism is the inevitable accompaniment of this pattern of development, though it is more formal and gentle, and initially requires an invitation or the permission coming from the African country (and her advisers).

The more entrenched a foreign country is and the more in-debted the African host country is to that foreign country, the much more difficult it becomes for the African country to exercise her independence and even control the activities of the foreign power to which she has virtually signed off a great deal of her sovereignty. The case is easily trumped up—to go and protect the life and property of compatriots in the African country on the premise that "law and order" (in the planned form) has broken down and something has "gone wrong with the occiput of the pig."

Most African governments sincerely regard, or like to regard, this "neo-colonial" stage as a "take-off" stage. They hope that in another two or three decades African countries will have wit-nessed the voluntary withdrawal of those who today control foreign monopolies and by then will have sold out their shares to African indigenes. In all optimism and providence this can happen; but would other foreign monopolies of perhaps even greater size and involvement not become successively necessary as development succeeds development in the far-advanced coun-tries and with continuing universal impact, craving and necessity? And would such development not continue to come and come into Africa in the decades that lie ahead, and in the same guise? It is doubtful, at the rate development is going, especially with the present gospel and pontification about capital promotion, whether Africa can ever escape from foreign economic domina-tion; rather she stands to become increasingly subordinated economically. The simple reason is this: Europe, America and Asia are not themselves static; they are dynamic, developing even faster than ever before. The vicious and perpetual circle of looking for this elusive and indispensable capital for African development can be broken only by a *giant Marshall-type plan* directed to the whole of Africa or large regions. The whole initiative for this can come only from united regions (or all regions) of Africa themselves, and not from Europe or else-where, even in all altruism. Yet these far-advanced countries and continents have an important role to play by offering their moral and diplomatic support to the various African countries. They must urge African countries to unite, as their only hope of economic emancipation. Unless African brain-power resources and personnel can be trusted to do things by themselves, even to make their own mistakes, African establishments will never be able to come into their own.

The earlier these facts are recognized by all concerned, the greater the chances of Africa's escaping from foreign economic domination, of Africa's diminishing the geometrically increasing gap between her forty-odd states and the gigantic regions of Europe and America which themselves are aspiring to even more gigantic economic entities.

The Irrelevance of Racial Equality

The major result of European economic domination over the peoples of African descent, both inside and outside the continent, has been racism.

Racial equality per se hardly deserves the attention being paid to it by various peoples. It would be worth quibbling about if any race spent a longer time in the womb or proved, on the average, to excel other races physically or intellectually or showed racial resistance to physical diseases and was exempt from mental breakdowns; or if it possessed, as a rule, extraordinary tastes, sensitivities and capabilities in respect of the five basic senses of touch, smell, sight, hearing and taste, while the sixth sense—common sense—was such as would prove infallible to members of other races; or if it possessed the ability to learn and to do what has been or can be proved others can never learn and do. Racial equality would be worth quibbling about if any race had any extraordinary ways of reacting to joy, sorrow and other vicissitudes of life in ways that can be regarded as superhuman or subhuman, never crying (or crying too often), never in sorrow or fear (or always joyful and foolhardy); or if it had not the same taboos and restraints as are generally recognized: for example, abstaining from eating certain articles of diet, showing unusual taste and longings for certain drinks and foods, for air and various liquids.

Indeed, normal human behavior and mentality in a healthy body are on the whole far greater blessings to anyone than the social consideration of belonging to this or that race.

Racial equality is important only in so far as it bears inseparable relevance to material prosperity, to affluence, to socio-economic security, in many parts of the modern world.

The people of European descent have now got to the stage where they have in their possession over 90 per cent of the hard currency for international tender within each of at least four continents, and this only within the last three centuries. As long as they continue to enjoy this incredible monopoly (in spite of their rather small over-all population) and as long as the peoples of non-European descent believe in wealth in exactly the same way as the peoples of European descent do, the non-Europeans will continue to feel unequal to Europeans socio-economically— ever longing for their favors, ever longing for their company, for their wealth and for their place, coveting, adoring and fearing these wealthy, unbeatable, lucky and purposeful people.

Racial excellence cannot be measured by material or industrial achievement alone. There are other factors which can in certain instances be a yardstick to measure human greatness. Either these are fixed or the living generation can hardly help their existence. Among them are geography, history, cultural wealth, social and religious practices, natural resources and economic potentialities. As such each race remains potentially great within itself, depending considerably upon its own sense of values.

Whereas economic rather than moral or racial issues lay at the root of the Atlantic slave trade and then of colonialism, so also do economic rather than moral or racial issues lie at the root of racial arrogance and racial bigotry.

Man is a materialistic animal, and even when he is deeply religious and would be called a religious animal, religion in this instance constitutes his own brand of materialism.

The principal contributory factor in racism and especially in racial oppression and racial suppression in all parts of the world where these occur is *deprivation* of what is material to the victims. The weak and helpless must be socially oppressed, not so much because they are hated or loved but because the oppressors have come to the conclusion that this was vital to their own very existence and any other cause is likely to end up in their eventual capitulation or loss of their insecure material hegemony over the oppressed. Myths are therefore evoked and elaborated. Discrimination, even by law and even in the house of God the Creator, follow in their wake. Discriminatory laws are framed which begin by excluding the poor, the ignorant, the illiterate—all of whom were probably preconditioned by their racial grouping against exercising their fundamental human rights, as if the others were congenitally invested with the ability to understand, read, write, display technical skill and grow rich.

It is most probable that if wealth and other opportunities for individual betterment were equitably distributed among the various races in these areas, there would be less racial apprehension, social intercourse would be appreciably improved and racial prejudice would be blunted. This must be one of the most imperturbable and humanly exciting phenomena on earth. There can be few things more self-reassuring and self-satisfying than to be able to get on quite well with everyone from anywhere on this planet, as if all were brothers and sisters born and bred in the same household. The magnetic curiosities and strangenesses found among the races of the world are often just as strong as the centrifugal forces engendered by the mistrust and insecurity due to the differences. Unfortunately human vanity and personal insecurity would not have it this way; people who would have been living in brotherly love—eating, talking and sharing each other's confidence—are polarized into perpetual warring camps, torn apart and seething with hate, mutual contempt and indignation.

In Euro-African dialogue all the opportunities for economic and social betterment, for fulfilling all human material desires in the modern world, are fully concentrated in the hands of peoples of European descent. Therefore vehement demands by Africans for integration, in Africa, America, Europe or elsewhere, are not so much for the company and fellowship of the European (which in itself is a very good thing) as more immediately for the only means of individual or collective socio-economic advancement or security in that particular area. If the apartheid policy of the minority government in South Africa, for instance, were such that Africans received an equitable share of the resources of that territory and enjoyed equal opportunities, even if these totally excluded political power, it is unlikely that these Africans would cry out so longingly for European fellowship, nor would the world condemn the South African European government so very much.

Suppose one of the races of mankind developed an entirely new form of power or any type of hitherto unappreciated or unknown power, be it derived from solids, liquids or gases, from the "natural" or the "supernatural," from plant or animal. Suppose this power were able to consolidate and propel the socio-economic security of that race to the point of even surpassing present-day science and technology in its potentials, its effectiveness, its manifestations and its usefulness to man's very survival, security and continuity—able to nourish, clothe, shelter, cure, defend and protect men and nations more than science today does—able to inject more conveniences, comforts and leisure into the lives of men and nations. In such a case there is no doubt whatever that other races—indeed, all the rest of mankind—if these decided to acclaim and copy and strive to derive the ends from this new power that the innovators themselves derived, would find themselves virtually at the mercy of these frontiersmen, whom they would covet and whose lead they would almost sheepishly follow as if here, in fact, were the only route to the security and salvation of men and nations.

The oppressive and agonizing apartheid policy and forced labor in Angola and Mozambique are a form of slavery still carried on. A minority group of Europeans hold millions of Africans in endless subjection and suppression, in incessant terror and deprivation, even in the face of the protest and condemnation of the world and in flagrant violation of the United Nations Charter and repeated resolutions. In the slave trade that lasted over three hundred years cardinals, scholars, etcetera, lodged their protests while efforts to encourage the trade were frequently made by theologians and biologists—Rev. Thomas Thompson (1772), *The trade in Negro Slave on the African coast in accordance with humane principles and the Laws of Revealed Religions;* Rev. Josiah Preit (1852), *A Bible Defence of Slavery*—and today similar influences are not found wanting, everywhere. The crimes continue, and the end is nowhere in sight. Instead the South African government grows stronger militarily and constitutes an open threat to the rest of the continent; the governments of Portugal and Spain are as adamant as ever and would rather not relinquish their strangle hold on their colonies in Africa.

Those humanitarian efforts in Europe that strive assiduously for justice and freedom in Euro-African dialogue do not seem to have received as much informed African support as they deserve. Some of the movements protest against slavery, against colonialism, against racism; some preach against this and against that injustice; some collect moneys for Africans on trial and sustain their families, offer scholarships and would fight the cause of Africa on various international platforms. The pressure groups who often arouse the conscience of their native soil to the misdeeds of a handful of their countrymen or those of other nationalities in Africa have no doubt rendered unforgettable and invaluable help. But one can little expect pressure groups in Europe and elsewhere to do more than hold protest meetings and pass resolutions in their fight for justice and fair play in Africa. Where economic problems are concerned, as is usually the case, these resolutions can only lick; they can hardly bite. Everyone knows full well that his own nation is itself deeply involved in the economic ramifications of the country he is accusing; and above all else, that Southern Africans owe (as ever before) their very economic existence and their national defense and their population level to the countries of Western Europe and North America.

There is nothing whatever, except man's desperate struggle for economic power and prolonged economic security, to show that the Europeans in South Africa or "Portuguese Africa" are in any way basically different in their reasoning processes, personality, morality and humanitarianism from those in Europe, or from any other human beings, for that matter. In any circumstance in which materialistic considerations become obsessionally predominant and vital, man tends to jettison all decorum and get into a prolonged unremittent and unrepentant rage. Few people guaranteed a life of freedom and opportunity in South Africa would refuse to go and taste of it, even when they are not prepared to accept the international leprosy attached to apartheid.

It is therefore not quite extraordinary that otherwise well-meaning immigrants ceaselessly go into these areas. Investments and "cooperations" and even arms—the very weapons of supression, and of perpetuation of European hegemony—continue to pour into Southern Africa under the pretext that they are instruments of maintaining peace and order.

Indeed, it is often wondered whether the various countries in Europe cannot oblige by repatriating their nationals of Southern Africa, promising to rehabilitate them, during which period Africans will be trained to take over the administration of this, one of the richest segments of the world, and the new Southern Africa will continue to trade with the rest of the world.

The real crisis is that some of the governments in the European world believe, consciously or subconsciously, that these unfortunate Southern African European settlers must be retained where they are, if they can stick it, as a reliable conduit pipe to continue siphoning off riches.

If political independence, with the attendant withdrawal of foreign domination, can be based on moral grounds rather than on the grounds of increasing African military might, can a case for racial exodus from Southern Africa, to remove the socio-economic domination of European settlers, not be made on moral grounds also?

The Europeans in Southern Africa cannot be easily dismissed

as immoral, nor would they be expected to be a truly happy, contented and hopeful lot. Rather they are a besieged lot—busy doing an altogether thankless job in our hypocritical world. The earlier a realistic answer and help can be given to them, the better for them and for their posterity and for the entire Euro-African relationship throughout the world. To repatriate about five million people in the twentieth century is certainly nothing to compare with the five million who left Europe for America just over a century ago. If all the Europeans in Southern Africa can be fully guaranteed socio-economic security on landing in Europe or in the New World, if they can be induced or persuaded out of Africa, it is doubtful whether they will choose to sit, even for another minute, on the keg of gunpowder at which racism and African nationalism are brandishing their embers. Ask them: all they will say is that they have no place to go to; no place to return to.

The thesis is this: the European population in Southern Africa can be bought out, if need be. This is not farfetched. As the sun of imperialism began to set in Africa around 1960, European administrators and settlers at various points on the continent were eased out financially—a burden shared by the imperial governments and the new African governments. Some of these Europeans were paid for "loss of service."

The Contradictions of Racial Integration

The slave trade apart, European colonial emigration into Africa apart, the peoples of African and of European descent continue to make increasing penetration into one another's territories, into one another's natural or adopted homelands. These movements increase as the century wears on. There are now many more people of European descent in Africa than there were before independence and more of African descent in European-dominated areas.

How do these movements of peoples in the present generations effect Euro-African relations? What are the prospects, in

the immediate future and in the decades ahead? Are these recent
and continued migrations actually in the best interests of peoples
of both racial stocks?

If it can be valid that their African forefathers were ignorant,
shortsighted and corrupt when they allowed or helped their
slaves and fellow countrymen to be carried away by people who
were complete strangers into some unknown oblivion, can
Africans of this generation plead, or expect future generations
to plead on their behalf, that they are just as blind, weak and
unthinking as their ancestors were in the Atlantic slave-trade
era?

What is of supreme importance to us of this generation is to
ask ourselves, individually and collectively, whether we are any
wiser or better than our ancestors of four centuries ago, who, in
collusion with the European slave traders and raiders, were party
to the shipment of Africans as slaves across the oceans—a tragedy
that has left its conspicuous and indelible scar on everyone of
African descent the world over. . . . Because we are living in a
different age, any crimes or any mistakes we may be committing
now, which may not only scar but severely maim our own posterity, are likely to be different in their nature and in their manifestations from those of our ancestors. The tragedy is that we may
not know. . . . Thus the necessity, once in a while, for a sober,
self-critical and penetrating analysis of our policies on the
African continent. . . .

Are we in fact today committing any capital and irreparable
errors in our enthusiasm for development? . . .

Is it possible to move faster—in the direction of greatness, and
not of ridicule? In any case, who is there to tell us? Certainly no
one without the same sense of deep involvement and without
our pattern of experience and background can truly appreciate
our legitimate aspirations with the same passion as we do. . . .

Whatever we do henceforth, no one of us must recklessly
blame the white man for any misfortune that may yet befall us
as a race: for all the time, ever since the first contact of the two,
any exploitation of the black by the white has derived largely
from the greed, selfishness and shortsightedness of the black
people themselves. . . .

The next few years may well be the finest stance the African

can ever dream of for a take-off. If, through our own human weaknesses, we alienate and frustrate the benevolence of our friends from other continents, the opportunity for a breakthrough may never again return. . . .

We must come out of the euphoria created by political independence to witness the phenomenal advances that are transforming human society. . . .[7]

Whereas during the Atlantic slave trade, Africans were taken away from their homelands with physical force and brutality, can it be said that certain forces exist today which, visibly or invisibly, compel Africans to go and live *under* rather than *with* peoples of Europe and America? What is the nature of the cudgel that seems to be driving Africans relentlessly and compulsively out of their own territories into Europe and the Americas?

People of European descent, mainly from Western Europe, have been emigrating into Southern Africa, and also into North America and Australia, into the last of which peoples of African descent are not allowed free entry. The European who goes to Africa usually goes straight into the middle upper class of whichever country he chooses, freer entry being allowed into the dependencies and those countries that have not yet tightened up their immigration policies. He would find it easy to receive help and favor from those resourceful Europeans who have already established themselves. On the other hand, the entry of the African into Western Europe invariably means he is to go straight to the lower rungs of the social ladder.

The European businessman goes into Africa to establish his enterprise, employing the indigenous African. It is he who, to a large extent, fixes the wages and dictates the conditions of service. The African often has little choice but to accept. Although the European entrepreneur would run his establishment in exactly the same way as in Europe or America, sell his goods at the same price as in his own country or even higher, he would pay his African employees only the salaries that would meet the local

---

[7] V. O. Awosika, in the *Daily Express* (Nigeria), Sept., 1964.

standard of living; yet dollar and gold both have a cruelly universal tender that does not discriminate between the poor and the rich, between the East and the West. On the other hand, countless inducement allowances are usually accorded to European immigrants when they work in the civil service or in other capacities in the countries of Africa. These allowances include those for children, cars, housing, servants, night watchmen, leave, and so on. Fantastic gratuities are paid on top of all these allowances which render the salary itself a handsome saving for the mouth.

The African is severely handicapped in this international relationship. Lacking the capital, the experience and the other prerequisites, he has no chance of establishing anywhere outside his own continent.

Most of the peoples of African descent enter Europe to seek employment, often as unskilled workers. Usually their case is that they were unemployed in their home countries or that they lacked facilities for education or that their countries were overpopulated; therefore they were encouraged by their home government to emigrate. Some of these people emigrate only temporarily into Europe, especially into the United Kingdom, returning to their homelands to settle. Some students, especially from West Africa, undertake part-time work to augment the insufficient funds they are able to obtain from their parents and relations back home. All these people enjoy relatively free ingress to and egress from Europe, and this is particularly true between the African Commonwealth countries and Great Britain, and was even more true before the British Immigration Act of 1962.

Some of the unemployed from the West Indies arrive in Britain with only a few pounds, or even after having made their journey on credit, but by dint of hard work and determination are able to possess a car or a house and enjoy a standard of living far better than they could have contemplated in their homelands. The same applies to some Africans. Some of these emigrants are able to send money home from countries of Western Europe. Their conditions of work, when they are able to get it, are usually the same as those of the indigenous Europeans, and they usually possess full citizenship and are accorded every aspect of the fundamental human rights, including freedom of speech and of association, which abound in the European host country.

Immigrants of African descent more often than not find themselves in menial jobs in most parts of Western Europe and America where they live. This does not imply that they are a deprived lot; indeed, they are always free to quit and return to their homelands. The significance of these much-despised jobs is, however, reflected in problems of racial integration in the countries of Western Europe—countries which are largely class societies.

Racial integration does not mean that peoples of different racial stocks—Europeans, Asiatics and Africans—live together as peaceful and agreeable neighbors. More importantly, it demands a smooth, harmonious, even effortless relationship in which peoples of different racial stocks regard one another as just other men and women, without any discrimination, with minimal prejudice and with the highest premium possible on merit and never on color, creed or country of origin, which in themselves can predetermine ability or merit. Racial integration is manifested not only in market tables or post office or bank queues and counters, but in every attempt which the individual may make to get himself established in society and to make his life as decent and as secure as any other person's. This means that he requires, a house, a suitable employment, a good school for his children; and that he can stand for election to the town council or legislature and partake maximally in business enterprises and in all social and welfare services, to the same extent as any other member of the community. His presence is accepted more as a matter of course than as a matter of tolerance.

Furthermore, for the immigrant groups to be adequately integrated into the established order, they must be fully eligible to take active and responsible part in the maintenance of law and order, in decision making and in administration; they must form part of the scaffolding, from top to bottom, of the national edifice. Thus integration is not a horse-and-rider relationship.

The racially integrated society or country is a comparatively new challenge, a new concept, even a new experiment, in human relations.

Certain factors enhance the success of racial integration in the manners defined above. First, the immigrant groups must have made up their minds to commit themselves and their future destiny to the new country and settle there permanently.

Second, the host group must have the *capacity* to absorb the immigrants almost unconditionally. The host group's capacity is a function of their patriotic homogeneity, in the sense that the Danes, with their long history, their monarchy and other national institutions and their language and culture, are less likely to absorb Indians and Africans than Australia or Jamaica, which are comparatively new, racially heterogeneous countries and with less distinctive language and culture. These areas therefore have a far greater capacity than Denmark.

Third, the social structure of the society—that is, whether it is a class society, as in most parts of Western Euorpe, as opposed to the Communist world and also to the new world, such as the Americas and Australia, even when there is much capitalism and plutocracy. (Most of Western Europe is fast becoming a classless society as the standard of living rises and affluence and opportunities spread to reach all citizens.)

Fourth, the immigrant groups must be adequately educated or skilled to enter the better-paid jobs; otherwise they will undoubtedly be forced to begin from the lowest rungs of the ladder. This in fact is the case with most Africans, West Indians and Asiatics in most parts of the European world.

Fifth, racial integration will be hampered whenever the immigrant group refuses to bow down to accept the shibboleths of the host group. This conservatism can be manifested in dress, food, language, names and religion, and these all tend to make social intercourse more difficult, especially if the host group tends to refuse to acknowledge the rights and aspirations of the immigrant group to persist in what it regards as part of its own distinctive personality. The possibility of immigrant-host marriages is thus as remote as ever.

When the helpless African victims of the slave trade landed on the Atlantic seaboard, their culture steadily withered, being despised amidst the hopelessness of their circumstances. They began to Europeanize themselves and to look upon the color of their skin with disdain. Richmond, reviewing the West Indian social pattern, noted—

A factor which gives the West Indian class structure its unique character is the association between these "middle-class values" and the high prestige of anything associated with "white" society. This is clearly a relic of the high status of white men and women in a society based upon negro slavery. While there is no absolute colour-bar in the West Indies today there is mild prejudice against the very dark person and occasional discrimination in hotels, clubs, and similar places. Nevertheless, the coloured man can, in theory, go anywhere, He can do so in practice as well, so long as he is obviously wealthy. The fact remains that the lighter a West Indian's complexion, the more acceptable he is in middle- and upper-class society. Colour values in this sense are extremely complex and the assessment of an individual's social status depends upon these, as well as upon the socio-economic factors usually associated with class differences. The concept of "colour" in this context is judged by actual skin colour and texture, hair formation, and facial bone structure.

The nearer the features are to the European rather than the African, the more they are approved. For this reason there is considerable demand, especially among the women, for the artificial straightening of hair and bleaching of the skin, to produce a "better" effect. There is a general tendency for those whose appearance is predominantly African to be described as "black" and to be associated with the lower class. At the other end of the scale are the European and the "fair coloured," who have the highest status. Between the two are the middle classes with a wide range of colour from dark to light. The fact that the terms used to denote colour are also social status symbols is illustrated by the fact that an obviously dark, but wealthy, person tends to describe lighter but poorer individuals as "Blacks." [8]

---

[8] Anthony H. Richmond, *The Colour Problem* (Pelican Books, 1955), pp. 233-24.

This may still be the case to some extent in the West Indies. With greater enlightenment, the general trend is for people of African or of Asiatic descent to pride themselves only on being themselves and to cherish their respective cultures and certain other social values.

On the contrary, the European on African soil has always upheld most of his ancestral standards and remained loyal to the European way of life. His language, his culture and his way of life are not only already thriving on the African soil; he finds it unnecessary to learn or partake in African indigenous culture and ways of life, partly because these are already withering away and getting steadily irrelevant. He therefore holds the African at arm's length. The natural result of this is exclusive racial residential areas, clubs, restaurants, schools, hospitals and other rendezvous.

Considering the five points raised above, it is all too obvious that racial integration is not an easy proposition in those European countries to which virtually illiterate and unskilled workers from the less developed regions of the world are emigrating. But there is a ray of hope. If the first generation of immigrants can be racially tolerated by the host group, with the children of these immigrants being given all the possible benefits of educational and other amenities in the host country, then real and gratifying integration is possible within the next generation or two. It will be hoping for the hopeless to expect true integration within a generation. All that can be done is for the host group to provide a reassuring climate that will make integration possible in the near future.

African students migrate into Western Europe and North America by the thousands in pursuit of knowledge. Most of them are less than twenty-five years of age. African children born in Europe and America begin their education in these countries. European and American countries have proved very helpful in providing places for these students.[9]

---

[9] It must be noted that the British policy has changed substantially of late. Overseas students are now obliged to pay much higher university fees than the indigenous British.

These students return to Africa taking with them the tenets of Western civilization and Western sense of values. They have learned from European teachers and developed a sentimental attachment, a gratitude and a sense of obligation to the institutions where they once studied. How far are the long stays of these students in the best and long-term interest of the African people? Have they affected the students' basic personalities? Have the students developed to the fullest capacity in an environment which is foreign, and away from their homeland? What are the possible consequences of having legions of this type back in Africa to occupy responsible posts and even shape the destiny of the continent?

If Africa is determined to develop in her own way, according to her cultural environment, and hold her own equally and forcefully, and maintain her identity in the face of other peoples, it will be essential to breed future leaders, during their formative period, in a manner definitely calculated toward these ends. Unless the African youth is deliberately oriented to cultivate certain national or continental aspirations, his education abroad may be out of step with that of his colleagues trained at home. Rather than being a well-groomed and culturally initiated African, he is more likely to become the type covered with the snow and ice of Western civilization, which could melt rapidly on his return to Africa, only to expose his nakedness.

To have African students staying abroad, especially in their pre-university and undergraduate years, is the first suggestion that the attempt must be made to acquire the same knowledge which the European student acquires. At best this does not put the African or Africa as a whole at a disadvantage.

The curricula in Europe are geared to meet local demands and passions. The ability to winnow out the sort of knowledge which will be relevant and useful to meet national or continental aspirations must be one of the great tasks before any government and its agencies. This applies in particular to the younger countries. It is doubtful whether the essential knowledge needed in Africa is the same as that needed in Europe, America or Asia. What is important is to sieve out what knowledge would be essential and useful to the healthy coexistence among the peoples of all the continents.

African universities have been quick to appreciate this fact, and curricula are now largely tailored to make them meaningful and relevant to national and continental aspirations. There is no doubt that increasing numbers of African students will need to travel to Europe and America for postgraduate studies and indeed on holidays and short holiday courses to have a glimpse at these countries and enlarge their horizons.

The Tireless Apron Strings

The evolution of the empires into the Commonwealth, the French community and the special Congo-Belgian relationship can be regarded as one of the greatest diplomatic triumphs ever scored in recorded history. Paradoxically these relationships would amount to an open vindication of colonialism. No one can have described the Commonwealth with greater authority than Gordon Walker: "There could have been no Commonwealth had there not been a British Empire. Equally there could have been no Commonwealth but for the negation, withdrawal and transformation of British Imperialism."

But the significant thing about the Commonwealth is neither the negation nor the transformation of British imperialism but the fact that this body had actually replaced the faded British Empire by the middle of the twentieth century. As soon as Nehru took India into it (a paradox, in view of his noble privations), it became almost a *fait accompli* that other Asiatic countries would graduate into this college from their colonial status. Exactly the same went for Dr. Kwame Nkrumah of Ghana, who virtually inspired the rest of British Africa into the Commonwealth.

It might be added, therefore, that "but for Nehru and then Nkrumah, the Commonwealth would not have emerged to what it is today: proverbial and multiracial."

As long as they continue to exist, in one form or another,

these post-independence graduate schools remain a feather in the old imperial cap, not in the cap of any of the other members.

These post-colonial associations are regarded as clubs for *equal* partners that draw no race, color, creed or culture lines. But it is at once obvious that the members are not and can never be equal by any stretch of the imagination; and the more so when votes are never taken.

Certain cynics, realists and political analysts have condemned these hangovers of colonialism as a gigantic farce, or extolled an organization such as the Commonwealth as the microcosm of the whole world and a feasible instrument of world peace. There is no doubt that the Commonwealth in recent years has confirmed these various points of view.

Be that as it may, no African country would actually delude itself into believing that because of its association with a mother country in Europe, an association that had involved so much bitterness over the centuries, it would deserve, by some form of poetic justice, to be specially favored, even in preference to some nearby European country whose territory was only a few miles away and with which the mother country had been sharing blood, cultural, political and economic ties long before it knew of Africa.

Similarly, no European country would expect an African country, unless in quite unusual and desperate circumstances, to rationally believe that it must be closer to a European mother country in preference to its African neighbors a few miles away which had been arbitrarily severed from it only within the last century. Their ancestors most probably belonged to the same medieval African empires, which existed long before Europeans set foot on African soil.

The Commonwealth is essentially British. The Commonwealth without Britain is a different proposition entirely, like Hamlet without the Prince, and it can exist, just like any other international organization, at times without a head or a principal convener. The Commonwealth remains unique and useful in so far as it is one of the most multiracial associations ever known; second, its members have become somewhat British, even more

British in many respects than those of British descent who emigrated into parts of the New World. The member nations have passed through the same crucible, have acquired all the sentiments of an old boys' association, speaking the same language, practicing or yearning for parliamentary life and generally leaning more to the West than to the East; its members have developed or acquired a certain common national outlook and adopted, in certain respects, similar ways of life, albeit very superficially and artificially.

The inclination to join the Commonwealth upon graduating from the school of colonialism represents a forward-looking, outward-looking posture and portrays the relative economic (and often administrative and educational) dependence of the former colony on the imperial power. That bad boy who agitated his countrymen out of the colonial status had got nearly all he wanted; now, being not so sure he can cope alone, in view of the manifold realities that are confronting him for the first time, he would like to maintain internal peace, stability and economic viability before he spreads his wings further. He would like to take his time in making new acquaintance. He would like to demonstrate to the world at large that his people are indeed capable of self-government. He wants to be saved unnecessary isolationism and possible bankruptcy. No wonder it has never crossed the American mind to belong to the Commonwealth, even though the United States once passed through the crucible of British colonialism and imperialism.

The Commonwealth bonds are durable, strong and genuine in so far as they exist between Britain and the old dominions, the so-called white or senior Commonwealth countries; otherwise, these bonds are tenous, feeble and unpleasant and do not bring back many happy memories. Yet they are and can continue to be very effective in the over-all interest of mankind.

The Commonwealth cannot and does not engender kith and kin in the sense that all members can feel equally proud in themselves that they belong; reservations are latent and indelible. The language cement which is often believed to be important in holding the peoples together is largely put on, for, apart from officialdom, the African, speaking for himself, speaks a totally different language from the Germanic nations and adopts the Germanic languages as a superficiality made compulsory by commerce and internationalism. Indeed, the English-speaking union, when all is said and done, is a far stronger and deeper force than the Commonwealth. The Commonwealth relationship is an immortal child of history that would have existed even without the sense of communion it tends to impart or perpetuate; it would have existed even without a name.

Conclusion

Africa is heavily dependent upon Europe and America for her development, if not for her survival. Europe for the past three centuries has been largely dependent upon the raw materials and markets of Africa for her survival and industrial advancement.

Africa is not any stronger in self-defense than she was four centuries ago, when she was completely subordinated by Europe. Africa is now relatively free; but is her freedom just a remission? Is another exacerbation of subjugation possible, or even around the corner? Africa is free because people of European stock have allowed it. The allowance is due mainly to their own contrivance. But what of world opinion? What of the Christian conscience? How far can these serve as a shield, if shield were enough, to protect Africa in case another invasion is imminent from any quarter, even from inside the African continent?

World opinion can be pooh-poohed by any power which conceives itself to be strong enough. This strength lies not merely in military or strategic power or in some metaphysical power but in economic influence. When a national economy is full of such ramifications that it can inflict incredibly effective blows on others, holding them at ransom, then that nation is powerful on this score alone. A glaring example is the Republic of South Africa.

World opinion is of significance only when the opinion of those who really count weighs mainly on one side or the other. There is no need to give illustrations here: the opinion of the forty independent African states can count only if they speak in unison. No one has ever been unduly perturbed at the alarming and disproportionate number of delegations that the African continent parades in New York. They probably suit the rest of world opinion better as they are: delirious, weak and faint of voice amidst the roar of opinions that really matter.

Turning to morality and the Christian conscience, how much can the African rely on these? Christian persecution had been known since the earliest times of the church. Indeed, Christianity has always been characterized by outspokenness. The Euro-African relationship has never met with any Christian persecution; rather it has been characterized by Christian connivance and acquiescence.

In most of Europe and the Americas where Christianity is the rule, it is commonly held that the church must not be allowed to interfere in politics. Should this, then, be acceptable throughout Christendom and especially in the Africa that received her first Christian teaching and her Christian orders from Europe? The stand of the church in international affairs is of great moment to the ordinary African, Christian and non-Christian alike. The church is one of the bonds that have united the peoples of Africa and Europe over the last four centuries. If the church is to be excluded from the Euro-African dialogue because it must not embarrass the home government in Europe or in Africa, it has virtually defeated itself, especially in Africa.

It would be grossly unfair to disregard the stand of the Christian church on such matters as racism, apartheid, poverty and disease, and of course the invaluable role the church plays in fostering Western education in Africa. Nevertheless, informed African opinion is of the belief that the church of Christ on earth should have done and should be doing a bit more to condemn, openly, crimes and injustices that were and are still being committed, in one form or another, in any country. The church, of course, has no military power; it can neither punish any government nor act as a policeman; rather, governments can banish church leaders. Yet the church remains the moral policeman, the accredited guardian of all morals, throughout the world, or at least throughout Christendom. How far the church should interfere in politics is a matter for Christianity itself to decide. If the degree of interference is dictated by politicians, then the church of Christ as it would have been constituted in Europe has no divine right to pontificate to Africa; if in Africa it is dictated to by politicians, it similarly has no right to discuss with Europe or indeed with anyone.

How far the individual Christian makes his own voice heard, even in opposition to his ecclesiastical superiors and even to the extent that he has to be silenced, or excommunicated, is an index of Christian courage and conviction.

Today, it is an open fact that other believers in the Almighty, the Creator who gives and takes all life, do visibly demonstrate their abiding faith in what they believe to be true and just; some go on hunger strikes and fasts or even publicly set themselves on fire in their effort to persuade, and to halt offenses against charity and justice.

Throughout the era of the slave trade and, again, throughout the era of colonialism the church remained conspicuously incoherent. Robert Delavignette remarks—

> We now come to a fact which must be indicated here, even if it cannot be explained. In the period when European colonialism was in full swing and controlled politically and economically huge numbers of human beings in Asia and Africa, the Holy See remained silent. No encyclical was published in the nineteenth century marking out lines of thought for Christians on the conquest effected by Europe and all that it implied. Why was there no attempt to transpose into African and Asian terms this admirable treatise [*Rerum Novarum*] which appeared in 1891 and ought to have illuminated the work of colonization just at the very moment when Africa had been partitioned at the Congresses of Berlin and Brussels? Here are one or two quotations

from it: "All the blessings of nature, all the treasures of grace belong in common and without distinction to the whole human race; . . . what is shameful and inhuman is to use men as vile instruments of gain."[10]

The fear of all African Christian soldiers is the relative acquiescense of the church. That racial discrimination can conceivably occur in places meant for the worship of God, even in areas where segregation has not been enforced by politicians, and that the church obviously is insufficiently coherent when Euro-African dialogue is involved in international relations, do not augur well for the promotion of the gospel or the integrity of the church in the world, and especially in Africa.

The problem is a perennial one. During the period of colonialism, factions broke away from denominations which stemmed from Europe. The church no doubt has the unique duty of fostering racial brotherhood throughout the world, irrespective of political or even religious beliefs. If those in ecclesiastical positions are called, it is not because they are able to speak many important languages or because they entered the ministry as teenagers and became professors, but simply because they have been able to listen and to hear the voice of God. It must be reassuring to all Christians, of all races and of all nationalities, to feel that they possess an equal sense of belonging, of attentiveness, and even of promise.

---

[10] *Op. cit.,* pp. 88-89.

CHAPTER FOUR

Racism: The Crisis of Nomenclature

Race Relations and Human Dignity

Workers in the field of race, scientists and humanists among them, have never been unanimous about the classifiaction of racial types. Perhaps the simplest classification would be into the three groups: the Caucasians—those who derive from Europe, as typified by the European of today; the Mongolians—those who derive from Asia, with the two great subdivisions into the Chinese and the Indians; and the Negroes—those who derive from Africa, as typified by the West Africans. There are, of course, scores of minor groupings and subgroupings—the Japanese, the Malays, the Arabs, the Australian aborigines, the American Indians and so on.

Racism has become one of the most formidable problems of our time. Never in history have peoples of all races been closer in many ways. With the emergence of independent nations in Africa and Asia, the necessity for even closer relations is bound to increase. Interracial fellowship is one of the inevitable ingredients of any national prosperity, power and influence. Therefore the problem of race relations is fast becoming one of the inescapable considerations of every single country, large or small, everywhere in the world.

But racism is not an insoluble problem. The ability of any

nation to cope effectively with the issues it may raise, comfortably absorbing peoples of various races, is usually a source of national relief and pride, and it is widely regarded as evidence of ultimate greatness and maturity, and of hope for mankind.

The origins of racial prejudice can almost always be traced to economic, political, religious and emotional factors. Whenever the physical presence of the minority group begins to constitute a palpable threat to the majority group, prejudices and apprehensions will also begin to make themselves manifest. This is common knowledge. These obvious factors nevertheless are no longer as intractable and significant as they would otherwise have been; the whole world is already quite conscious that they exist and that they are very unhelpful. Furthermore, the world today strongly advocates human dignity, justice and brotherhood, and condemns oppression and persecution in all forms and guises.

It is not the intention to discuss the concept of race here. Suffice it to say that it is a very complex phenomenon which involves anthropological, biological, sociological, cultural, geographical, historical and even political considerations.

Racial discrimination and racial prejudice are different concepts.

Racial discrimination is a resentment focused on a whole group. Its most extreme form is represented in the apartheid policy of the European minority government of South Africa.

Racial prejudice is personal. It is unofficial and quite independent of any group decision or governmental legislation; it simply reflects the mind of an individual to another race. In racial prejudice the mind has prejudged the personality, ability, attributes and all the goodnesses and evils of the members of another race as a group. Even before any confrontation or communication takes place, the mind, to all intents and purposes, has practically been made up.

Yet it is only natural and human for us to have our various prejudices, to have our own tastes. But tastes are often best developed only after a series of firsthand experiences. Legislation against racial discrimination not only promotes firsthand knowledge but makes this knowledge possible, so that the assessment of the other races can be made at first hand, more accurately and unbiasedly. When, however, the tongue has already been heavily coated with gall or honey, the sense of taste cannot remain a reliable and fair assessor; indeed, it can be worse than having no such sense at all!

Whereas it is possible to legislate against racial discrimination, a purely sociological issue, it is impossible to legislate against racial prejudice, a purely psychological element. It is, however, possible to eradicate racial prejudice by educating the mind, by deliberately or circumstantially orienting it. It is especially possible to accentuate racial prejudice by similar processes.

Racial prejudice is usually regarded in the negative sense. Strictly speaking, there are instances in which one of the races in question can be especially favored in the attempt to placate or reassure its members. This is not necessarily an act of patronage or arrogance. It has more to do with the sense of justice or the attempt to create a reassuring air of assimilation, integration and equal (creative) opportunity for all and sundry in the given community. This incidentally is one of the unfortunate dilemmas of human relationship, for it can often be relevant. Yet it often is terribly difficult to say whether there are prejudices for or against an individual in any given instance. It would appear that some people often prefer the easiest way out: they would not like to involve themselves in racial problems at all; they would not like to see any such problems on their doorsteps. Into what category can one put these people—reasonable, defeatist, fight-shy, insecure, diffident, incapable of grappling with the inevitable?

Yet in an ever-shrinking world no one anywhere can successfully avoid the bizarre challenges posed by nature in the diversity of human racial types.

No comprehensive picture of how economic, political, religious and cultural factors influence race relations will be painted here. The world has witnessed and still is faced with so many wars fought mainly over any one of these factors, it is unnecessary to devote space and time to discussing the significance of each one of them.

By far the most vital factor in any attempt to solve the deeply involved problems of racism is the promotion of mutual understanding and mutual respect among peoples of different races. This will alleviate the problem in certain countries *immediately*. It will also help in setting a solid foundation for the future, by diminishing the development of prejudices and suspicions, especially in childhood. The attitude of the mind must be given considerable attention so that the stereotype of other races is as fair and as near the true picture as possible in everyone's mind.

Even when all economic, political and cultural factors have been adequately appeased, the most fundamental issue of all is human dignity, and the consciousness in the individual of each and every race everywhere of that dignity. Human dignity must be guaranteed and credited to each individual of every race, and it must not be wantonly challenged or trampled underfoot.

What, then, are the things that undermine human dignity, with particular reference to race relations? It is not necessarily the injustices pertaining to politics and religion or to one-sided distribution of economic resources and potentialities. On the contrary, these injustices themselves may have originated in the first place from mere denial of human dignity. Again, it is not necessarily whipping, forced labor, physical assault or physical insult that undermine human dignity; nor is it necessarily those fervid attempts by scientists to prove racial superiority or inferiority by measuring brain weight, skull circumference and other physical data. It is not necessarily the films, etcetera, which in the name of entertainment, rather than of ridicule and humiliation, vividly portray primitive life, portray man in the worst form of human or even in subhuman existence. It is something far closer to earth, something far more mundane, ordinary, yet virulent: *the words regularly spread by mouth in everyday life in various parts of the world in human relations. These words not only reflect attitude of mind but also help in the making up of that attitude.*

True, the media of mass communication have never been so

effective on the mind as they are today, and increasingly so tomorrow and even next year. Theirs is the incomparable task of controlling feelings and prejudices, projecting and adjusting images of all racial types everywhere. No one and nothing can conceivably do these better. A joke on the screen or radio on a Christmas Day, for example, can frustrate all the built-in efforts for a happy day for members of any race anywhere. Television in particular can be unnecessarily awkward to host and guest alike whenever more than one race are gathered together: certain programs are better avoided so as not to embarrass an otherwise perfect evening of cordiality and fraternity.

Yet the power of words, spoken or written, seems to have been grossly underestimated and sadly neglected in the over-all question of race relations. The reason for this is perhaps understandable: the languages of interracial currency—English, French, Spanish, Russian, German—are all European.

Europeans (perhaps including all peoples of European descent settled outside Europe) are the inalienable custodians of these languages. To them all other peoples of the world are more or less obliged to regard whatever emanates from the European oracles as the accepted or the acceptable or even the final word. That this should apply preordainedly to words in regular use in race relations therefore must be regarded as a very unfortunate incident indeed, the more so when peoples of European descent are now leading the whole world in practically every aspect of material human endeavor (including world administration); the more so when they are in full control of all the scientific means of disseminating any new information or new knowledge. Moreover, they are in inexorable and continuous contact with the peoples of African descent in at least four continents.

Nonetheless, these languages are no longer the exclusive prerogative, or the monopoly, of peoples of European descent. As parts of culture they can be learned, as tools of knowledge they can be deeply understood by all, to their minutiae, and as vehicles they are used to communicate and to transmit the impressions of the mind. Furthermore, these European languages happen to form the lingua franca and the official language in many countries outside Europe.

Words can often be directly personal or rendered so by simple inference. They can have profound emotional impact on an individual and leave their unfavorable and indelible impressions on the mind. One may use a word which appears harmless, or which one believes would not be harmful because it is the one in popular parlance, yet that particular word may, to some other people, prove offensive and insidious. Whether or not the word in point is regarded as an offense depends not so much on the rawness or thickness of the skin as on people's intelligence and their ability to interpret the word in relation to the circumstances in which it has been used.

Innuendoes apart, uttered words can become unduly offensive merely by making certain variations in the emphasis and intonation of the component syllables. Certain words can mean different things to different people at different places and even at the same or at different times. Language, changed perhaps unavoidably and perhaps for the sake of its very survival, must continually be enriched. But we hardly can hedge. We must always say what we mean. It is dangerous to do otherwise, even if it entails the use of many words to express what is on our mind. In race relations it is far better to err on the side of terminological exactitude than on the side of oversimplification or laziness. To use words just because they appear simple and indeed when they are actually oversimplifications is to begin to oversimplify the very intricate problems of race relations.

It is a bitter irony that the key words in frequent use in race relations do not in themselves enhance free and smooth discussion between peoples of different races—a sina qua non for any form of racial understanding, whether at the summit level in international politics or in the more intimate and informal personal relations. Most of these words would often do nothing but fan the flames of racial prejudice and create unnecessary, unfounded and unfortunate animosities. Some of these words tend to foster racial complexes and racial bigotry. In Euro-African relationships the best-known are *colored, black, Negro, Negress, mulatto, half-cast, expatriate, European, African, American,* and various combinations of these. All these words, some inveterate, hallowed by long usage, appear in print and on the air whenever references have to be made to peoples of African or European descent in various parts of the world. It is also significant to note that they either receive straight translations into other languages, like Finnish, Hindi and Chinese, or are interpreted as above, from the more popular European languages, such as English, French, Spanish and Portuguese, into thousands of other languages.

How proper, valid or logical are these terminologies, conceived by anthropology, biology, history, geography, politics, complexion, ignorance, laziness, bigotry, contempt and hatred and born into a world of make-believe? The courteous and enlightened person of any race, if and when he stops to thinks about it, would hesitate to use some of these words even in reference to the deaf, the insane or the very young, believing they must be improper and repellent. No one, anywhere, ever seems certain which names to adopt. The confusion is often ridiculous and even pitiable. It attains its most astonishing pitch of inconsistency and chaos whenever a news bulletin includes racial strife in the United States, British Guiana (Guyana), Southern Africa, etcetera. Well-meaning and reputable correspondents, commentators, reporters, preachers, teachers, diplomats and friends of every race, in their decency and candor all begin to falter, stutter and meander for lack of suitable words of reference to peoples of the various racial groups concerned once a geographical name or the nationality cannot immediately convey all the meaning and make the point. Language suddenly becomes clumsy and unutterable. An otherwise frank discussion becomes so inhibitive that it sinks into a shallow and even insincere performance in a genuine attempt to avoid touching sore spots and causing eyelids to bat.

By *common usage* one means that an expression is used officially in law, in the press and in public discussion. This must be differentiated from such obvious abuses as nicknames, which are never of course official.

"Colored"

This epithet is used in many parts of the world to refer to those born of union between two racially distinct persons—for example, only one parent being Asiatic, European or African. In this sense it implies a miscegenation.

In the Americas and in the West Indies, in the earlier days of their colonialization, to be a colored person automatically conferred a higher social status on the individual than if he were just a pure African or a pure red Indian. In Southern Africa the Cape coloreds enjoy certain social privileges over the ordinary African or Asiatic. The epithet colored is also used in certain countries, especially in the West, as a simple collective term for all peoples who are not wholly of European stock. In this sense they are colored in so far as they cannot be grouped as "white."

The word colored can amount to an abuse, not because one particularly wants to interpret it as an abuse but because its connotations are most unlikely to have a favorable impact on the mind and are therefore detestable. These connotations include *stained, spoiled, discredited, enriched, badly punctuated, interposed, impure, false, flavored, embittered, marred,* to mention only a few. It is at once obvious that the word is a handy adjective to describe a variety of materials or events or anything of any shape or consistency, animal, vegetable or mineral. Moreover, even when it is used without any disrespect, this epithet is bound to create an odd, unusual and bizarre image in the mind: the "colored" individual is seen through tinted glasses for a long time before his true color can eventually emerge, if ever.

This apparently simple and useful epithet commonly used in race relations asks far more questions than it can ever attempt to answer. What is color? What is not color? Who is colored? Who is not colored? Is anyone or any color colorless? Colored in respect to what? *What* is colored? What parts are colored, and with what color? Is any color standard? Is any particular color *the* color? Anywhere? and so on. In any case, before *colored* can become logical and acceptable in race relations anywhere it must take regard for the majority in the particular area, and any color that does not conform with that of the majority will automatically be regarded as the odd one out and be termed colored. The epithet colored is a preposterous one. It seethes with contempt and arrogance and does not warrant being used. It becomes more distasteful if the individual wishes to be dissociated from miscegenation, for this may be a basically detestable thing in itself, perhaps unreasonably so.

The epithet colored is immediately riddled with racism, urgently mobilizing all available prejudices and suggesting that such differences as are in existence *must* be made manifest. The emotional impact it creates is better felt than imagined or described.

On the social, collective or political scene, *colored* can be a rallying force, either within a country or internationally, but such a force is not usually toward the improvement of fellowship among all racial types. The epithet assumes an even more obnoxious moment when used as a descriptive or possessive adjective—*colored world, colored matron, colored prime minister, colored vote, colored conscience, colored lives, colored blood, colored quarters.* It is doubtful whether any so-called colored persons anywhere, including those of "bi-racial" parentage, feel happy about the word. But why do they not say so? Why do they acquiesce? Would their immunity to being so called mean an indifference, even to the extent that they would refer to themselves as being colored? Would such a nonchalant attitude, such pent-up indignation, help racial harmony anywhere? Even if they are immune to this epithet, what emotional impact has this word got in race relations? Has continued usage of the word any effect on the user or on the person of whom it is being used? Does it not matter at all? Is the word colored indispensable? Is there any alternative? And lastly, is there in fact anything in a name?

Anthropological Classification

NEGRO

Negro is derived from the Latin word *niger,* "black." The word has been used ever since the earliest European came across the indigenous peoples of the coasts of Africa, and before the birth of any systematic study of anthropology, much more before anthropological study became universal. It is to be noted that Darwin propounded his theory on the origin of species in the nineteenth century, not so long ago, during the slave-trade era and that he probably was influenced by the trade in his theory. Whoever was the first to use the word Negro, in anthropology to describe the peoples of Africa had no deeply scientific or well-informed rationale to do so, as it was only very vaguely descriptive of color alone among the several distinctive features of these peoples. Furthermore, the various colors of peoples of other races were never given a similarly prominent consideration in ascribing to them their scientific names.

In several ways European-inspired education unduly correlates the peoples of African descent with the anthropoid apes. There is no doubt that these are hangovers from the pommeling of the last four centuries.

Biology demands comparison of the various species of beings. In an era in which the sciences are increasingly being taught in schools all over the world, it is important to mention the potential menace which scientific classification can constitute to otherwise healthy human relations.

Comparative anatomy stresses the parts of the human body which bear close resemblances to those of the great apes in every kind of human being, for example ears, jaws, hair distribution, lips, limbs. All these correlations are facts which are easily confirmed by anyone, even the uninitiated. Unfortunately, as in all branches of scientific knowledge, peoples of European descent have emerged the greatest authorities on these fascinating subjects. The nomenclatures in use can often lead the non-European only toward self-depersonalization and self-abuse, and it often does not need a perspicacious mind to understand their often outrageous inferences. In many instances the data presented are in fact unconvincing; the influence of such factors as environment, climate, nutrition and disease has never been and may never be fully known.

A prominent example which has to be accepted by all students of midwifery or biology is the classification of the human female pelvis into four major types. The anthropoid type is reported to be found in all races, but the majority of Negroes are alleged to possess this type of pelvis, while the other three types of pelvis are predominantly found in other races and only occasionally in the Negro. It is the African who wants to fail his examination who would omit to learn this type of classification and swear to it in his written or oral tests, even to African examiners. Weights and dimensions of several organs of the human body have also proved of considerable interest.

As science advances and man is split into his elements it becomes of utmost importance not to allow racial whims to impair the joys of scholarship and knowledge.

As the Negro mounted the world stage in mid-fifteenth century one of the first arguments to be raised was whether he was a man as such or whether indeed he was not subhuman—a debate which attained to an intellectual bonfire on all sides of the Atlantic, with various papers being read for and against in certain cities of Europe in the attempt to defend the slave trade and still the conscience of all and sundry. It was under the darkness of these thick clouds which pervaded Europe and America that the slave trade was perpetrated for centuries, with all its atrocities and dehumanization. This discussion was prolonged to the instance of Adolf Hitler, if it can be valid to quote him, who in *Mein Kampf* (1939) claimed "it is an act of criminal insanity to train a being who is only an anthropoid by birth until the pretence can be made that he has been turned to a lawyer."

If Europe had not conquered Africa, and had not ruled Africa, the tendency and the readiness to associate the African, more than any other types, with the anthropoid apes would have been far less and not quite so distasteful or contemptuous. Had the European biologist arrived in medieval Africa, before the decline and fall of man, he probably would have developed his classification differently, appreciating the high degree of social and cultural organization of the people. Thus the image of the African grew steadily worse in European eyes, based on the slander, fabrication and ignorance of merchants and seamen as part of the myth to perpetrate their crimes. So far as Europe knew, she was to be content with regarding the peoples of Africa merely as Negroes, of some indefinite status in the animal kingdom, and when they arrived in Europe, they were to be regarded as "noble savages," children who needed to be trained, for they had no culture, no vocabulary, no philosophy, were incapable of abstract thinking and had no knowledge of their physical and biological environment. They were innately inferior, with a low intelligence quotient, etcetera. This stereotype of the "Negro" was developed everywhere; and superimposed upon it were the woes and humiliation of the slave trade and of the total subordination of colonialism.

Today and forever it is impossible for anyone anywhere to dissociate the stereotype of the Negro and the slave trade within his own mind. It is equally difficult to think of the man and of the Atlantic slave trade which was abolished over a century ago without remembering vividly all the humiliation and dehumanization that occurred. In most of Europe and in the New World in the days of the slave trade, *slave* was inevitably synonymous with *Negro*, "that Negro" meant "that slave," and "that slave" meant "that Negro," until it was proved that the slave in the European mind, and especially in the mind of the New World, was not in fact an African, at least in part, but European or Asiatic in whole.

This psychological aspect of the hangover of the slave trade affects people of European and African descent almost equally. Used out of anthropological context and in correlation with other racial types, the word Negro in mid-twentieth century is patently an unfortunate anachronism.

Psychological emancipation into the reality that emancipation of the slaves indeed occurred at least a century ago, and emphasis on the fact that when groups of Africans today voluntarily emigrate into the Americas or the West Indies they are unlikely to be called Negroes as such are essential factors in promoting the best relationships among the peoples of African and European descent everywhere in the world.

It is a comparatively easy proposition to accomplish emancipation by legal means and by assiduously correcting political, economic and social factors resulting from slavery. But it requires far greater pains and even mass psychotherapy to exorcise the image of slavery from the mind. No one wants to be ignorant. No one wants to be unforgiving. But the worst things are best forgotten if only for one's daily life and happiness and also for the good of future generations.

The term Negro is wrong, and it will never be meet and right as long as it lays undue emphasis, exclusively, on color, while the colors of other races are never given a similar pride of place among all their own respective racial characteristics. Here we meet with incontrovertible evidence of the double standards that would not translate brown, white, pink, yellow and other shades into Latin and put them into universal use.

Admittedly Negro in reference to the black man is an age-long epithet. Suppose the coiners of this word never chose, as they did at the time, to lay emphasis on the striking color of the first natives of Africa they met but chose to call them something else—rags, niggers, woggs, pigs, Afros, demons, ciphers, chairs, spades or whatever. Would the world continue to accept these terms up till today? At best there is no reason to suggest that their acceptance would have since been revoked. Ordinarily it might not be wrong to use Negro to refer to the black race, but the same breath must necessarily choose exactly equivalent categorization for the other major races.

Again, to use the word Negro if this were indeed an acceptable anthropological term, to describe those of African descent, it smacks of the double standard not to use the equivalent anthropological terms in reference to peoples of Caucasian or

Mongoloid races. To use *Negro* for Negroes exclusively and scientifically, even in speaking ordinarily anywhere, while other races pass under some other cloak, is by itself another evidence of discrimination.

The emotional and psychological effect of this unfortunate double standard, bequeathed to us by our ancestors of previous centuries, attains its most striking degree when news headlines or subheadings, and even ordinary conversation, have to make mention of the clash, marriage, cooperation, etcetera, between peoples of African descent and peoples of European descent.

What impact can the following newspaper headlines or subheadings have on the mind: "Negroes and Whites Clash" "Negroes and Police" "Mr. Thomas meets the Negroes"? The objection attains a new nauseating pitch when *Negress* is used; *tigress, elephantess* and *lioness* leap to mind. The mind subconsciously reduces man to animal status. The abuse is as complete as it can politely be.

But again, who are the Negroes? Are they the Africans on the west or east coasts of the continent or are they the descendants of those Africans of the fifteenth to the nineteenth century who emigrated into the Americas and the West Indies? There has been substantial admixture of blood among the different races in the latter areas, and the Negroes are roughly those whose racial appearance, skin color and hair texture, singly or in combination, appear closer to those of Africans on the west coasts rather than to those of Indians or Europeans. Using these criteria, only about 30 to 40 per cent of the so-called Negroes in the United States would unquestionably look like Africans south of the Sahara. Moreover, in Africa itself, and especially to the north of the Sahara region, there are palpable Berber and Hamitic influence, which will not pass for black or Negroid.

It is also claimed that at least 30 to 40 per cent of those called Negroes in the United States have pronounced Caucasian blood in their veins. These people, in other countries, will qualify as *colored, mulattoes* or *mestizos*. Others elaborate the confusion by recognizing American Negroes, West Indian

Negroes and African Negroes, and before the end of this century there will be Negroes in certain other places. The term Negro will then vary with geography, and the criteria for becoming a Negro will also vary from place to place.

Blanco (Latin, "white") is a word analogous to Negro which is well known in parts of South America.

Both these words, blanco and Negro, lay undue emphasis on skin color, albeit illusory, delusory or derisive, and take no account whatever of other racial characteristics.

MONGOLIAN

The classification of the Asiatics into Mongolian, or Mongoloid, races is inept. Of particular significance is the connotation which the word Mongolian has when *mongolism* is used to describe the children's disease Down's syndrome—a congenital condition characterized by mental deficiency or idiocy, and changes in the eyelids, facial appearance, hands, feet, etcetera.

An appeal to change this embarrassing terminology was thus aired—

SIR:

It has long been recognised that the terms "mongolian idiocy," "mongolism," "mongoloid," &c, as applied to a specific type mental deficiency, have misleading connotations. The occurrence of this anomaly among Europeans and their descendants is not related to the segregation of genes derived from Asians; its appearance among members of Asian populations suggests such ambiguous designations as "mongol Mongoloid"; and the increasing participation of Chinese and Japanese investigators in the study of the condition imposes on them the use of an embarrassing term. We urge, therefore, that the expressions which imply a racial aspect of condition be no longer used.

Some of the undersigned are inclined to replace the term "mongolism" by such designations as "Langdon-Down anomaly." or "Down's syndrome or anomaly" or "congenital acromicria." Several others believe that this is an appropriate time to introduce the term "trisomy 21 anomaly" which would include cases

of simple trisomy as well as translocations. It is hoped that agreement on a specific phrase will soon crystallise if once the term
"mongolism" has been abandoned.

Gordon Allen, Maryland; C. E. Benda, Massachusetts; J. A.
Book, Sweden; C. O. Carter, England; C. E. Ford, England; E.
H. Y. Chu, Tennessee; E. Hanhart, Switzerland; George Jervis,
New York; W. Langdon-Down, England; J. Lejune, France;
Hideo Nishimura, Japan; J. Oster, Denmark; L. S. Penrose,
England; Pe. E. Dolani, England; Edith L. Potter, Illinois; Curt
Stern, California; R. Turpin, France; J. Warkany, Ohio; Herman
Yannet, Connecticut.[1]

In support of this opinion, seven weeks later another letter
appeared, from Dr. Charles William Durn of the Hospital for
Mentally Retarded, Stockley, Delaware, suggesting "congenital
submental and somal deficiency syndrome" as a possible substitute for the "oppressive" title *mongolism.*

CAUCASIAN

The term Caucasian (or Caucasoid) used to describe peoples
of purely European stock is inappropriate in so far as the *-asian*
in it can easily be confused with *Asiatic.* This term is the least
used of all anthropological classifications, not only in ordinary
conversation and in officialdom but also in scientific literature.

Geographical Classification

There has been so much human migration, especially in the
last two centuries, that it has become almost impossible to define
whom exactly we have in mind when ordinarily we refer to
Africans, Europeans, Americans, Australians. Nevertheless, a
European, at least to those who are neither European nor of
European descent, and to those who do not intend to be too
patriotic or parochial, is the European or the European descend-
ant still in Europe or settled in any other part of the world.

---

[1]Letter to the editor of the *Lancet,* Apr. 8, 1959.

In this context, again, there are references to the American Negro or the American Indian; but we never hear of American-Mongolian. Euro-American, Americo-European or anything akin to these is almost unheard of. As such, *Americans* as applied to the white people of the United States is either an oversimplification or a presumption—the presumption that those of African or Asiatic descent are relegated to the background and count for little or naught in America, which may be a misrepresentation of the fact.

It is easy to understand these grievous anomalies and appreciate that no harm is primarily meant. It must be noted that among those of European descent, since it is they who control the languages and nomenclatures, as it were, they are at most times speaking only among themselves while non-Europeans are merely eavesdropping. The tendency is to draw international and interterritorial lines only among themselves as Europeans or descendants of Europeans, largely ignoring their fellow countrymen of other races. But this can no longer obtain. All races and all citizens everywhere are not only acutely attentive of but also partaking actively in all deliberations and discussions.

Skin Complexion

It is always amazingly difficult to give a definite name to the color of any human skin, much more to the skin color of two human beings, far more to the skin color of a whole nation or a whole race. Therefore the average is taken, and then it is just as tedious as ever to ascribe any definite name to it. To compare the average color with the color of some article of diet or of some plant or of some well-known manufactured material is to heap confusion upon confusion. The simplest way out was to pick upon black, brown, red, white and yellow in the attempt to describe peoples of different races. It is doubtful whether anyone can produce the human being that will approximate to these colors as known to the physiologist and the milliner alike.

These blatant oversimplifications, terminological inexactitudes or illusions would have been apt if only in order to give a convenient distinction between the various groups; but unfortunately this is not and can never again be the case. Some of the colors have certain malignant and obnoxious connotations which are bound to adversely influence the psychological factors in race relations.

These epithets severely prejudice racial harmony, especially between the peoples of European and African descent. The two groups popularly known as black and white, respecitvely, are the furthest apart in the spectrum of human pigmentation.

Cyril Bibby[2] sees the Negroid color as ranging from "virtually black to quite pale yellow-brown; while their eyes and hair are commonly brown or black." He sees the "Caucasoid" as being "not white; their skin color ranges from pale pink to a deep ruddy hue, from a pale olive color to a definite brown. . . . Just as their skin color may range from pale pink to dark brown, their eyes may range from pale blue to deep sepia, and their hair from almost white to black."

Black-and-white photography gives variable chromatic impressions of members of these two groups, but it is in color photography, movies, television, etcetera, that the truest pictures are painted. Therefore it is obvious that the premises on which these colors are founded are quite tenuous.

Although white does not need to be snow before it is white, yet no one human skin, as contrasted to the teeth and the scleras of all human racial types, is white as we ordinarily accept the white color to be.

The so-called white skin is often at least as near to pink, cream, putty, beige, yellow, golden, albino, red, brown or café-au-lait—or nearer—as it is to white as we know this color to be in ordinary descriptions, as in paint or in the shop.

Again, although black does not have to be ebony or anthracite before it is black, no one human skin color, as opposed to hair colors in most races, is black as we generally accept the black color to be.

---

[2] *Race-Prejudice and Education* (Heinemann, 1962), p. 11.

The so-called black skin is often at least as near to dark brown, light brown, yellow, slate, dark gray, blue-black or beige—or nearer—as it is to black as we know black to be in the day-to-day description of materials we all know.

The so-called black people and the so-called white people are, as groups, only light and dark in relation to each other. There are lighter (some say fairer) shades in the "white" group— the blonds; there are also darker shades in this group—the Mediterranean types. Similarly there are lighter (some say fairer or yellow) shades in the "black" group, and the darker shades of this group are the nearest to black or to dark gray or to dark brown.

Black is, or perhaps has merely become, about the very worst word in English and in most other European languages. The more versed one is in these languages, the more he becomes aware of all its connotations. Black is an adjective, and is therefore applicable to almost anything describable: weather, career, materials, diseases, strikes, institutions, activities, etcetera. Black represents the worst side of anything conceivable. It is also used in such obviously sinister yet useful and handy expressions as *blackleg, blacklist, black sheep, black market, blackmail, blackguard.* The list is a long one. Besides, there can be no end to having new words with equally pernicious connotations.

When the word black is used to describe people, it cannot possibly carry as much favorable impression as may be intended. Perhaps this is why many people would rather avoid using it. It is usually used along with other colors, for example, *black and white*—and never in such contexts as *Europeans and blacks* or *Indians and blacks* or *Police and blacks.*

Other colors are only very seldom used except in such contexts as *Red China,* and here Red stands more for political color than for anything else.

In contrast to black, *white,* the symbol of purity, virtue and everything that is good and noble, has apparently lost all its malicious and objectionable connotations. Words such as *white slave, Whiteboy* and *whitecap,* and expressions that involve fright, death and anger have virtually disappeared from common use; they are never heard on the radio or seen in the press and therefore are not used colloquially.

What impressions has the word *white* in human relations? What is the psychological effect or the emotional impact of white in reference to someone in expressions such as *white man, white complaints, white quarters, white lives, white vote, white conscience?* The full impact and psychological effect of using *white* and *black* are brought home when used together as adjectives in contexts such as *white and black quarters* or *white lives and black lives were lost.* In most African countries the word white is never used officially and the tendency is to use *European* for anyone whose ancestors must have been European, for example, Americans and Australians of European descent.

Certain African languages, even though they possess the word white, never use it to describe the European. They would rather use descriptive terms that often connote *pale, faded, red, discolored, tanned* or *burnt.* The informed African is unlikely to describe any European as white without genuine reservations: first, the European in the hot African climate is of a darker hue than he was back in Europe; second, the word white is inappropriate and inherently abusive.

Words such as gray, blue, pale and dark are also in use, depending more on the state of health than on any other factor. They need only be mentioned in passing.

The cardinal questions are: First, do the relentless references to white on the one hand and to black on the other have any effect on the mind?

Second, does the usage of these two words accentuate racial complexes—invoking contempt, ridicule and innuendo on the one hand, while on the other they evoke respect and righteousness?

Third, do these two words inspire, manifest or encourage, consciously or subconsciously, racial complexes and racial bigotry?

Multiracial Descent

MULATTO

This word is derived from the Spanish *mulato,* which means a young mule. A mule is the offspring of a mare and a he-ass or of a she-ass and a stallion. When this epithet is used to describe those born of biracial parentage, the unmistakable and mulishly animalistic undertones of the word render it abominable in every sense.

When females are accorded the epithet *mulattresses,* the insult spills over. Therefore those who know the deeper meanings of these words hardly ever use them. The victims of such epithets cannot be expected to welcome them if they know their origins. Yet these customary insults are found in many discussions, books, films, etcetera. The so-called mulattoes are often addressed in these terms to their face when in fact no harm whatever is meant.

Mixed race and *mixed blood* are in fact expressions also used for people in this group.

The word *mixed* connotes confusion, impurity, impregnation, adulteration, amalgam, and the like. The word mixed, when ascribed to race or to blood, to say the least calls for "wholesomeness" as the standard and throws into the open the whole question of miscegenation. Moreover, the word mixed can quite easily be confused with marriages between members of certain churches or religions, such as Catholic, Protestant, Jewish, Muslim.

HALF-CASTE

This is a deplorable expression because of the unwholesomeness it depicts, and *caste* is not a polite word by any stretch of the imagination. The whole expression grows in absurdity as the victim himself matures in his years; for a man in his seventies it must be a terrible burden indeed.

Mestizos is a similar word in use in South America for people of biracial origin.

"Expatriate"

This is an old word which sprung up during the closing years of colonialism in parts of Africa to describe all non-Africans. It is still in use in parts of English-speaking Africa to describe all, including people from neighboring African states, who do not belong to the country in question. Its use is practically confined to officialdom. The word is objectionable in so far as it can hardly be dissociated from careerism. Where they are bona fide citizens, how much sense of belonging, patriotism and permanence can be expected from people so categorized? It is patently an expression of unwantedness and is bound to instill a sense of social insecurity.

Settlers is used to describe Europeans in areas with substantial European population who have decided to stay in Africa permanently.

There are many other epithets in use in areas and instances which involve peoples of African and European descent. Obvious nicknames and abuses will not be mentioned, but it is important to appreciate that the terms now in common use most probably originated as nicknames.

It is unfortunate that some of the nicknames have now become customary insults. Millions of people in various parts of the world have got to put up with them throughout their lives— to be born into them and to die by them.

It is impossible to estimate or exaggerate the amount of unhappiness which the usage of some of these words can cause, the wounds they inflict on the mind, and most importantly, how much they can readily poison, perhaps for life, associations which should otherwise be cordial and harmonious.

To all the above is being added a new menace. Recently, in certain countries, dissatisfaction with some of these words has manifested itself in official circles. Words and phrases are being modified and even officially authorized to meet political and other local considerations. Kenya disallowed the use of *blackmail*, and substituted *redmail*.

There is no doubt that race relations become even more precarious when expressions that are in universal use, even when they are not universally tolerable, can entrap the unwary foreigner ignorant of local etiquette.

The danger inherent in the use of color was brought home by the expression *white blacklash*, which featured prominently in the United States election campaign of 1964. This expression soon metastasized into the subsequent British election. The expression *black backlash* came into being, and soon began to resound in certain other countries.

How long will this crisis of nomenclature last? Certainly, language must change, and in so doing keep pace with social, economic, political and other factors. Some of the words are decidedly obsolete, and any attempt to perpetuate them can only continue to court resentment and aggravate racial apprehensions in many countries. Only a world that would condone racism would condone the continuance of some of these words and expressions as they are now used in various countries and in various contexts as outlined above.

If it can be part of human standards and conventions to seek out and condemn pornography, vulgarity and heresy, and if while we lustily extol and cherish free speech in all countries, we are still prepared to recognize certain words as being unparliamentary or rude, would it not be possible to set up an international body to remove these unfortunate, ubiquitous and difficult anomalies and downright misnomers which serve no purpose but to foster racial prejudice and animosities in various parts of the world? This is a problem that must concern sociologists, linguists, semanticists, anthropologists, psychologists, psychiatrists and politicians alike.

The fate and happiness of humanity should no longer be subjected to the slander and jest of centuries gone by nor allowed to remain in the hands of zealous journalists and brash humorists.

There are manifold difficulties. There seems no easy way out.

But the more outspoken the whole world can be on this very basic and universal problem, the wider will be the scope of interracial and international understanding. Should the world continue to acquiesce in or ignore this intricate yet fundamental problem, it will never achieve the rapport and mutual understanding that are prerequisite to genuine friendship.

It is not so much that one can be personally abused in a foreign country but that in the spirit of the biblical "whatever ye do unto my brethen, ye do it unto me," any misfortune that befalls groups in one country may re-echo in widespread disgust, disturbances or even war in another country. The possibility of a War of Jenkins Ear being fought on this sort of basis alone is therefore a real one, the more so in a world which has been compressed into a tennis ball by the phenomenal powers of science.

A government cannot be fully responsible for a verbal or physical insult occasioned a visiting head of state by some irresponsible persons, yet this can have grave consequences in the visitor's home country, even within the hour.

Conclusion

It is one of the very saddest aspects of life and yet one of the most intriguing, challenging and exciting that the world should contain peoples of different races, and at the same time that these peoples should be almost equally capable of palpable degrees of innate dignity and pride which remain imperishable and almost indomitable in spite of any psychological, economic, political and other pressures that might be brought to bear upon them from within or without.

Migration is a politically loaded topic which has been deliberately left out here; it can fill volumes. It is bound to achieve increased importance as the present century wears on.

It is clear that with growing self-consciousness with cultural conservatisms and tenaciousness everywhere (and in spite of an inexorable trend toward internationalism and interracialism in many respects) peoples of all races are getting so increasingly committed to remaining essentially themselves that even if a scientist were to discover some drug to turn all peoples physically into a single racially distinct type, no matter which one, no one would unreservedly undertake this mutation, even by an iota, however safe it might prove.

Again, miscegenation no longer confers the type of social benefit or honor it did in the earlier days of the New World. Today miscegenation occurs not so much because it is the preferred thing, for if it were a possible phenomenon that a child of biracial parentage should emerge completely uniracial, that is, completely African or European or Asiatic physically, then interracial union or marriage would probably be a far commoner practice.

There is nothing that can sometimes defeat a man so helplessly as the simple fact that he belongs to a certain racially distinct stock. He has nowhere to hide. He is either present or absent. He has to stay to receive the mud or the confetti that will be thrown at him in a particular instance. All his potentialities—physical, mental, and artistic—are locked up within his skin. It will matter little at first whether he is of good or of bad character. It will matter little whether he knows or is ignorant, whether he is capable or incapable. Be he actor, entertainer, sportsman, professor, politician or cleric, so long as he belongs to the wrong group in a given place, he can still be quite detestable. This is the most terrible tragedy of racial prejudice.

To look at one's own child and imagine it will inherit all the problems of racism, perhaps in a more intractable and unpredictable way, whether in its attempt to live in its fatherland or merely sojourning in other lands, is to shake one's head and admit a major defeat.

Humanity is at a crossroads. The problem of human brotherhood should be a challenge, not a tragedy. It has been presented to man by nature, by God. Whatever the human being can ever be capable of achieving—he may reach for the moon, live a healthy and prosperous life span of two centuries, roll in wealth —as long as his life can be punctuated and molested by racial hatred, as long as he can never predict what next may happen to his child sojourning in distant lands, as long as his radio and television throw up disquieting news from some other countries about people who are being persecuted just because of the racial stock which he shares with them, he can never guarantee his own happiness and peace. He is led to conclude that at best he is in a cocoon of his own making, unable to fly out, as a matter of course, as a universal brother-beloved, a citizen of the world, to just anywhere his heart yearns for, even on a brief visit.

A careful revision of the obsolete terms is imperative. They are now eminently absurd. What is the point of calling a person a West Indian when he definitely is not an Indian? Who is a Caribbean? Geographical names must be made for the convenience and not for the confusion of men.

It will be important to seek the agreement of a people, in the light of all relevant factors, to the names which they deem fits them best. The name must be regularly reviewed in terms of changing political situations and other factors. Otherwise the name accorded them becomes simply a nickname or customary insult and an unmistakable instrument of interracial psychological warfare.

CHAPTER FIVE

African Assertions

The Human Ego

It is one of the basic characteristics of man to assert himself. The fact that he has presented himself at all, rather than withdrawn shyly, is a manifestation of this self-assertion. His past experience, his will power, his self-confidence, his potentialities, his hopes and aspirations, are all involved in his attempt to register his presence.

Human assertions are a part of human vanity, yet they are part and parcel of the ego. They are capable of defiance, of magnanimity, responsibility, compromise and also a sense of justification. These assertions are manifested not only by individuals but also by groups—families, clubs, ethnic groups, nations, races and so on—who represent, albeit subconsciously, a part of the greatness which they choose to lay claim to.

Apart from man's innate desire for a long and prosperous life, he desperately desires a kind of immortality. He wants to be immortal in a special sense. He would fight with death, and before he was physically dead, like to ensure that memories of him would last for as long as possible, even forever. He would like never to be forgotten. Again, in the subconscious effort to perpetuate himself, he reproduces his own likeness in his children. He shows up at different places—to witness, to meet people and partly to let it be recorded that he *is*. In modern times he takes photographs so that his reflections, even at a particular moment, can last forever.

The African in the world of the second half of the twentieth century must be acutely conscious of which things he must assert, and why he must assert them. He must be equally conscious of what he cannot afford to assert. If the African neglects to assert himself, he faces complete obliteration of his soul. He will steadily depreciate until all inside him fades away. He will find himself devaluated, depersonalized and reduced to a helpless, hopeless and hapless human shell. Henceforth the function of this cipher *here* would be merely to stand aloof and watch those who have bothered to assert themselves continue to do so even more vigorously.

The slave trade over, the lease of life allowed the African was never terrible enough to completely emasculate his spirit. By an unyielding and determined assertion, the right to control his destiny in his homeland was restored to him. This was a victory for his self-confidence, his hopes and his aspirations.

With the same spirit, finding himself a full member of an ever-shrinking and aggressive world, he decides once and for all to launch himself on the scene and declares for himself his own individuality and his own uniqueness, as expressed in the African personality.

His cultural heritage is an irreplaceable gem and a deeply sustaining factor which must live on, unspoiled and imperishable, as an indispensable armament to be bequeathed proudly to his posterity. His cultural heritage must last forever.

It will be unrealistic and decadent for the African to assert all he has in his arsenal. He must discard what in his considered belief are obvious trivialities and useless anachronisms which might impede his political, economic and cultural progress as a citizen of the world. He must cooperate with the forces of incorruptible and just internationalism and contribute his own quota to the over-all greatness of human society.

There is an intense struggle for survival in culture. Culture is presented with pride and hope. It is presented or even advertised with the wish that it will be honored, cherished and adopted, wholly or in part, by others.

Man is steadily becoming a helpless slave in a world heavily charged, managed and threatened with scientific and technological advances. Everywhere, and in many ways, culture is being affected by these advances.

The African already stripped to his pants found anything that looked like cloth acceptable enough to cover himself. As the African was emerging from the immediate consequences of the slave trade, with severe retardation on all fronts of human aspiration—the fall and the fragmentation of the pillars of culture, dwindled manpower and a gravely disrupted socio-economic order—the European was arriving, fresh, from a highly organized and robust region.

The colonial European was little interested in asserting his culture as such, except where this promoted his central objective: trade. But whatever was left of the African mind and morale had become all too susceptible to anything new, bright or beautiful.

In so far as Europe had in fact conquered Africa, it would be ridiculous to accuse the imperial powers for any spread of their cultural influences.

Whereas within the confines of European culture in which advances in science and technology are taking place, several aspects of European culture can be carried forward and even nurtured, this is not so true of other cultures. Indeed, the chances are that science and technology, used as a direct vehicle for spreading European culture, and the European culture itself, rendered even more attractive, will surpass, obscure or even erase other cultures, albeit unwittingly. Of all non-European cultures the most susceptible victim is African culture. Should Africa lose her cultural heritage, the consequences would be immeasurably great, affecting Africans everlastingly.

Yet Africa must surge forward with the rest of the world in the age of science.

Already Africa has lost unfathomable and in places irretrievable ground so far as her cultural heritage is concerned. Unless she recovers, and recovers rapidly, she will never again be able to regain, and then maintain, a position of honor and sincere respect in the comity of nations and races.

Always and everywhere the African, rather than presenting ambitious carbon copies of others, must, as distinct from others as others can be distinct from his, have something to offer to other people. He must have something original and which will reflect his own honorable background and his own identity as clearly as others do, in order to invigorate and perpetuate himself. He would take in return only when necessary.

It is perhaps a sweeping generalization to talk of an African culture as such. Nevertheless, it seems that in every aspect there is a continuous connecting thread that links the various ethnic groups on the continent together as if they all belonged to the same levels of intellectual, emotional, perceptual and creative development, which differ from those found in Asia, Europe and elsewhere.

One of the painful and important questions of this age is, How much can be salvaged and perpetuated of African art, sculpture, drama, music, song and dances, literary and oral traditions, dress, political and religious institutions, customs, ethics, sports and leisures? Furthermore, how steadfastly can these withstand the hurricane and the magic of foreign cultures in an ever-shrinking and science-obsessed world?

Should the zest to protect and cherish so-called African culture be so intense as to take precedence over the more urgent need of the ordinary African in the street—the fight against disease, ignorance, abject poverty and misery? Is the almost inordinate desire of the African elite for the resuscitation of African culture a manifestation of his own vanity, repletion and sophistication? Is it a jingoism, an absurd, misplaced and mistimed approach by an enlightened, forward-looking citizen amidst the intractable problems that stare Africa in the face? Or is it a manifestation of constructive and realistic patriotism?

Would it serve the African better if he totally and brazenfacedly rejected his own culture, languages, traditional way of life, customs and indigenous institutions and then cast all his lot, all his talent, with European or some other virile and attractive culture? Can he, for example, seize European culture out of European hands, capitalize upon it, strive to improve upon it

and use it to his own advantage, even to the admiration and
envy of Europeans themselves? After all, what is left of African
culture? Most of it can be said to have largely disappeared into
the limbo of history and social anthropology. The languages are
all retreating daily; and for practical purposes most of the customs, traditions and institutions are increasingly becoming rather
useless or trivial in a madly changing world—a world which
itself is getting inexorably materialistic, scientific, telescopic and
microscopic.

All these pertinent questions are easily dismissed as follows:
First, European culture has already developed into a fashion
which has become so prohibitively expensive that none but the
richer countries can afford to sustain it—either economically or
with scientific and technological know-how. For these reasons
the African cannot be truly fulfilled within European culture.
Furthermore, it is doubtful whether African authenticity, crea-
tivity and depth can attain their maximum pitch in a context
which is extrinsic or at best adopted.

Second, European culture truly and strictly expresses what is
European, and it would be a pity if what should be truly African
cannot be similarly expressed, if only for the blend and fullness
of human wealth and possibilities.

Third, European culture is not a prerequisite for African
socio-economic advancement. For the African to adopt it blindly
and wholesale would be to the detriment and eventual obliteration of the African personality.

Africans, like peoples who belong to the other cultures, can
borrow from their cultures, accept science and technology, which
strictly is not part of any culture, and march forward socio-
economically, thus improving themselves while nurturing their
own cultural taproots, which they must never lose.

A great deal can still be salvaged of African culture. Resuscitation is still possible on many fronts. It must be noted that effective European cultural presence in Africa is still less than a
century old, and in fact can be officially dated from 1885, when
European languages and recognizable patterns became the
establishment in each colony.

The European Impact

European penetration into Africa in recent centuries has been accompanied by cultural influences as well as by the blessed and fascinating fruits of science and technology.

The European arrived with his language, his way of life, his impressive ceremonies, formalities and brand of etiquette. He arrived with all the institutions of his native land—political, civil, economic, military, educational and so on. Indeed, the European arrived generously and conservatively, with everything he had. European foods and drinks and thousands of items of commerce soon trickled into the remotest corners of the Dark Continent.

For the African a new era had arrived! Whoever created this and that must be powerful! He must be infinitely wise, efficient and wealthy, and highly advanced! It must be wonderful to emulate him! There and then the African began to slip downhill. Henceforth he was to despise all things that belonged to him—they were cheap, worthless, useless, inefficient, clumsy or ineffective. Europeanism became a piece of advertising. Any locally produced article of good quality passed for European-made or European-imported; articles of poorer quality were dismissed as local, cheap or counterfeit.

In private and personal life, to copy the European in attire and in general fashion became a mark of social distinction.

In public life, program and procedure at ceremonies and at business meetings began to assume the European pattern, with all its hallowed punctiliousness and ritual. Even menus and drinks in some cases. The African, especially the copycat elite, had discovered a new and easy resourcefulness in his ardent quest for the European way of life. In doing so he often killed his own originality and even his own intuition. Steadily he began to despise his own cultural heritage and himself.

By the twilight of colonialism only those areas with strong Muslim influence had been able to resist painless erosion by European culture and also withstand the prestigious associations and persuasions of Christianity. Elsewhere paganism and animism had succumbed quite easily to the Christian faith. Arm in arm with this faith came Western education, Western tastes, dress, languages and national institutions, all of which soon made their visible impacts. All these, of course, had their own beneficent values. Again, as the sun of colonialism began to set, European cultural influence, propelled by European education (in places where this was not deliberately suppressed), varied proportionately with the degree of social advancement achieved at any particular area on African soil.

Fired by the political and economic implications of the European presence, leaders of public weal and leaders of thought soon began to see the dangers inherent in total acceptance of European culture. Africans who had been abroad to study and those who had been to other continents during the two world wars, strongly reassured their people that their ancestral culture, too, had its wealth; it must be invigorated, not despised.

Racism in colonial Africa added its own quota to these misgivings. Africans in the civil service, who felt they had *all* the right to belong, were often embarrassingly turned out of clubs, hotels, hospitals and other rendezvous patronized by European immigrants. Gradually the African elite, angry, frustrated and in personal revolt, began to divest himself of the top hat, the tail coat and other articles of Western outfit.

This sort of reaction was most pronounced in British Africa, although the British were less concerned with local traditions or with policies such as the Portuguese *assimilado*, which sought to invoke the Portuguese out of the African. Up till today, it is an open fact that Nigerians and Ghanaians, for example, tend to be less British than the Senegalese and the Congolese, who are respectively French and Belgian in their ways of life.

Most educated Africans no doubt hold European culture in high esteem. The more enlightened the African, the more clearly he realizes that he could never become a European in theory or in practice. He finds greater promise, reality and fulfillment in himself as an African. Should he attempt to graft himself onto European culture, as if it belonged to him naturally, he would actually be undoing himself. If, on the other hand, he is able to borrow discreetly those aspects of European or some other culture that would embellish his own culture, he stands a far better chance of getting his own culture and his own ego invigorated.

The African must readily and wholeheartedly accept science and technology to develop his continent and to enrich and protect himself in the modern world.

Science and technology, if they have to be included in the complex of culture, must occupy only a very secondary place. They are relatively shallow. They do not represent a spontaneous expression of the texture, depth and cultural wealth of any people or nation as such. Rather they are achieved, after prolonged concerted effort and experimentation, by any group of people who have received specialized training. Science and technology are the by-products of man's ambition to conquer or to reconcile himself with his environment. Arts and all other aspects of culture, on the other hand, are expressions of the deep feelings, humor, esthetics and sensitivity ingrained in man.

Again, science and technology are unrepresentative. They are not peculiar to any group of people definable by their language, history, nationality, environment, genetics or race; rather they are easily learned by all, and they create a degree of response or curiosity in those of any group who have not already been initiated into them.

The message conveyed by science and technology can be understood, felt and appreciated by all, irrespective of their background or exclusiveness. This is not so true of culture.

The peoples of Africa are of course capable of achieving a breakthrough (albeit with the help of non-Africans) into science and technology, which, in the name of humanity, belongs to all and is of great benefit to all. But never in the same way can they achieve a breakthrough into European or any other culture. They can continue to pursue foreign cultures indiscriminately only at the cost of ultimately losing their own cultural identity and self-consciousness, irretrievably and forever.

Imitations and Adaptations

Man is capable of imitation to an incredible and almost limitless degree. Imitation includes all types of learning, the adoption of various institutions, aspects of culture and ways of life, and so on.

Any two persons can mimic each other, and the degree of perfection varies with their sex, physique, race, personality, and intelligence and other traits. But there is a limit to which imitation can be carried. At a particular stage it becomes stupid, ridiculous and unbecoming.

If it has to be resorted to, imitation can be so successful as to amount to a triumph of common sense and brilliance, earning genuine respect from all onlookers. Originality, on the other hand, when it can be separated from absurdity, is always fascinating and will always meet with a degree of appreciation.

For one to voluntarily imitate another is the first evidence of insufficient faith in one's own way. On the other hand, whoever feels he is being imitated tends to feel a sense of self-righteousness and pride.

Since the beginning of history, civilizations have always been spread by conquerors' enforcing their will upon the vanquished, whose ways of life can sometimes be radically altered to suit the whims and caprices of their masters.

Civilizations and cultures were spread in Europe in earlier centuries by conquest. This process was far easier, logical and healthy than the penetration of European culture into Africa in recent centuries. The conquered races in Europe had little difficulty in becoming assimilated into Roman, Greek or indeed any other European culture: the contrast between the conquerors and the vanquished, between the rulers and the ruled, was never exceedingly sharp. They were often quite similar economically and culturally. Social intercourse was not difficult. They were all more or less racially homogeneous, even though their tongues differed.

In modern times the penetration of European culture into the Americas and Australasia was not arduous. The immigrants soon outnumbered and defeated the original inhabitants, who then steadily diminished in numerical proportion.

For Africa, with the incursions of European culture in this age, the situation is strikingly different in many respects. Here two sharply distinct races are involved—the Caucasians and the Negroes. Africans are most unlikely to be outnumbered by Europeans on the African continent, very much less to be assimilated into the European stock.

It is true that Europe has ruled Africa and that the imprints of Europe there will last for an indefinite period. Today practically all aspects of life in Africa are visibly influenced by European experience. Political, economic and cultural institutions of the various African countries today all derived to a great extent form Europe. Several modern institutions in Africa such as parliament, the civil service, universities, industries and hospitals, are all carbon copies of the imperial pattern. But only further research into African history could exclude the probability that these institutions did not flourish to a greater or lesser extent before the arrival of the European, in the days of the great African empires of this millennium, or even earlier. Be that as it may, the reality is that on the individual level today—and it will be increasingly so tomorrow—most of the personal belongings and a substantial fraction of household belongings found in Africa have derived their diverse inspirations from Europe. Most of the modes and methods of sports and leisure are copied from European experience and of course all that belong to the realm of modern science and technology. All these have now become almost indispensable to Africans, especially those who are reasonably prosperous.

As a result, when the African talks of "development" he does not limit himself to food, clothing, shelter and relationships within his tribe. Rather, he begins to think more in terms of a highly organized society with elaborate division of labor. He aspires to attain a standard of living comparable with what he has seen elsewhere or heard about.

As the African goes to study in countries with strong European influence, he comes into direct contact with European civilization. He gains an insight into European or Euro-American culture. He feels it, tastes of it, more or less gets absorbed into it. He measures it and compares it with anything akin to it back in his home country.

In his personal ambition to achieve the "world class," he must promptly internationalize himself, far more quickly and more drastically than his European colleague, who is already more or less as internationalized as he needs be in a world in which science and the essence of socio-economic development are overwhelmingly dominated by peoples who belong to or who originate from European culture. He must learn hard, and faithfully, to belong honorably to the new age in Africa and in the world. He must learn science, economics, agriculture, law, other subjects. As his link with his own African environment steadily weakens he is inexorably absorbed into the Western fabric. Not only must his first name be agreeable to the tongue and his attire adjusted to meet the demands of his profession, his office or society, but his language also begins to melt away, and all that belonged to Africa gradually ebbs away from him.

On returning to Africa, the "trained" African has acquired new or even strange habits and routines. His possessions, his occupation, his taste and his way of life are very different from those of his immediate ancestors, who had been busy farming, petty-trading or doing next to nothing. Now, in this new setting, he lives more like the European in Europe than like the average African in Africa.

How happy within himself can this type of African be if he stops to assess his situation within the context of his less privileged relations and neighbors and also when in the company of his European colleagues in Africa? This situation is worse than he found in Europe when he was a student. His European colleagues and even some of his fellow countrymen who had been abroad merely continue to nod their approval or make their polite corrections and suggestions as to what is "right" or what is "wrong" by European standards or ethics. He would receive similar instructions from his own people, even though these would hero worship him.

Deep inside him he must feel torn between two worlds to neither of which he wholly belongs.

Soon he finds certain adaptations necessary; he finds something to lean back upon—his own cultural heritage. Through this he is able to make his life more real to himself and respectable to all and sundry. He finds his own people are not so difficult to get on with after all, provided he shows he still belongs to them and essentially to the culture. He also discovers that his European or Asiatic colleagues respect him the more for this attitude.

To spread one's culture is to spread one's will power and one's influence. The African would like to see some aspects of his own culture—language, dress, literature, music, social traditions—penetrate as deeply as possible into other peoples' cultures. It is only when cultural exchanges are bilateral that they can be mutually constructive and engender mutual respect. But for African culture to become suitable for export, Africans themselves must be the very first to show their abiding faith in it.

The obvious fact that the African often has to make carbon copies of various aspects of European culture, either as a carry-over from colonialism or as a component of national development, must be a contributory factor in European reassurance and European pride and a root cause of racial arrogance and complexes.

The African Personality

By *African personality* one tries to bring into sharp focus what the place of the African is, should be or must be on the world stage in relation to other, equivalent personalities—for example, of Western Europe, India, China, the United States, the Soviet Union—collectively and severally. What is the African comprehension of world problems: the quest for peace, prosperity, human dignity, human brotherhood?

Any objective study of the African personality must assess it as an ideal and also assess the concomitant, its impact on the world scene.

There always has been and there will always be a form of African personality. This consciousness was first manifested to the world in the late nineteenth century when the Pan-African Conference met to challenge the deliberations of the Berlin Conference, at which the imperial powers carved out Africa among themselves. This spirit endures until this day in the existence of the Organization of African Unity. The consciousness that there *is* an African personality as distinct from other, equivalent personalities, is an effective armament ensuring that the African will not be depersonalized or devalued in the eyes of the rest, that he will not lose his intrinsic identity and his more human values in his unbridled quest for a life of prosperity and materialism; he must continue to exist even in his zealousness for interracial or intercontinental orchestration.

African personality represents the sum total of African past experience, present knowledge and judgment. It represents African attitudes toward the realities of the modern world. Africa's wealth and manpower resources, Africa's self-criticism and self-confidence, Africa's hopes and fears, her constructive assertions—courage, vigorousness and ambition—all these factors predetermine Africa's rational approach on various issues. They will also determine the effectiveness of any African approach in world affairs.

This is all well and good, but what is the actual power and resourcefulness of Africa? What is the quality of the peoples of Africa, as individuals and as groups? How do other personalities regard these?

Surely Africa's size, population, economic, military and political strength would, all together, predetermine the reaction of the world to her. Therefore, how is Africa as a continent with its resources being guided and guarded by political fortunes and military strength. What are the brain-power and manpower resources within the continent that will project the image of the continent abroad and fulfill its purposes and its aspirations? What does the individual African think of himself at home? How does he feel in himself when he is abroad and in contact with other personalities? What is the stereotype of the African in his homeland in the minds of non-Africans in other parts of the world? And what do they think of him when he gets out of his continent to confront these other personalities?

All these questions can be of paramount importance in international dealings of any category: summit, student, diplomat, industrialist, clergy and so on.

The performance and achievement of the African at any international meeting will depend upon his own individual personality as well as on anything that he has for presentation, be this an idea, wealth, policy, performance, art or culture.

The personality of an individual has much to do with his appearance, his physique, his intelligence and knowledge, his self-confidence, his background, personal experience, adaptability, wit and other endowments. Some of these factors are partly inborn; others exist in relation to socio-economic environment.

Here it will be sufficient to deal only with those aspects of the personality of the African individual which specifically relate him to his European contact and the rest of the world at large.

PHYSICAL APPEARANCE

How far must women go to make themselves look attractive? What areas of the body must a woman cover up with cloth, and how thick or thin, tight or loose, must the dress be in the various areas? There cannot be an easy unanimity anywhere on all these vexing questions. Any such unanimity will vary considerably with local ethics, religious beliefs, governmental intervention and so on.

In European and American countries issues such as these are always quite freely discussed. The level of social advancement, public interest and outspokenness probably encourage such discussions. Opinions and attitudes in these places tend to vary appreciably with prevalent religious and governmental influences, with affluence, and with the degree of what is generally regarded as sophistication in the modern world. Films are censored and graded, and attempts are made to prevent the public from exposure to whatever, in the opinion of the government or some other constituted authority, would amount to obscenity, nudity or pornography which might adversely influence mental hygiene or national life.

In Africa, however, the dilemma is of a different nature. Here the individual sometimes displays how tragically he has become entrapped and confused between two different cultures.

While in most European countries certain cosmetics are freely used by grown women, the tendency in certain African countries is to discourage the use of these articles. This is not for economic, religious or political reasons, but because those in authority find these cosmetics distasteful and vulgar.

The same can be said for certain makeups and outfits which are purely a matter of personal taste and the unfettered manifestation of such taste, however tolerable or intolerable that taste may be.

This dilemma multiplies itself and looms very large in an Africa where youths and even the elderly are heavily exposed—through what they see around them, through their visits abroad and compelling modern advertisements—to outfits, appearances, cosmetics and sophisticated practices which are obviously foreign to the indigenous life on the continent. Should African men, for example, have their thick, richly coiled hair straightened? Should African women wear scarves, hats, wigs? Should they curl and set their hair like European or Asiatic women or should they have them plaited? Should they paint their lips, fingernails, toenails? When does the African begin to copy the non-African to the extent that he not only exposes himself to infuriating ridicule but also constitutes an intolerable embarrassment and actual nausea to his own people?

DRESS

Dress is not only a means of identification, it also serves to indicate moods, such as joy, sorrow and ceremony. It can also be used to convey casualness. It is a means of projecting pomp, culture and personality. Furthermore, dress is a means of expression and thus can have significant impact in international or interracial relations. No wonder newsmen and commentators often go to great length in describing the dress of celebrities and royalty on august occasions. Again, in all walks of life, from the holy orders to charlatans, in institutions such as universities and the armed forces, in clubs and societies, everyone tends to dress to meet the occasion. Often the weather or the climate is decisive in choosing which dress to put on.

The African dilemma in this age is, How far can he judiciously go in copying various modes of dress for use in those institutions which themselves derived from Europe or elsewhere? How appropriate are these modes of dress or uniforms in the African environment: climate, economic resources and social ethics? Are the obvious differences of color of skin, and even other, subtle physical differences, guiding factors in choosing not only the color but also the style of Western dress that have to be used in the various institutions? Most of the institutions are completely novel to the new Africa, yet these institutions must hold, or come into their own, in the modern world. African universities wear undergraduate gowns and expensive hoods which vary in their distinctions and faculties as commonly as they do in European and American universities. Is this practice in the best African interest? Certainly there are African indigenous materials which can be developed to serve as academic laurels: garments, hats, neckwear, walking sticks, ornaments, flywhisks, etcetera. Any of these truly African articles would probably be a greater treasure to the celebrated non-African academician or nobility upon whom an honor is to be bestowed than just another richly embroidered robe bearing the sales mark of the guest's own home country—returning coals to Newcastle.

Whether Africa needs to make any special attire available in her academic, religious, legal and certain other institutions is one salient question. Another question is whether Africa can provide such attire, and ornaments, as will be distinctly African, thus invigorating Africa's cultural background and selling African culture to the world.

In civilian life it would seem that African women, especially in West Africa, have been more conservative and insular, as Asiatics have found, than their men, who tend to be more international in their attire—even to the extent of wearing tail coat, top hat and all that would normally be expected on a ceremonial occasion in Europe or North America.

In some parts of Africa, European (or international) influence is vivid and often bewildering if not absurd: articles such as top hat, morning trousers, jacket, Panama hat, shirt and laced shoes are mingled with indigenous items.

It is natural to cherish certain aspects of one's ancestral practices; yet whenever these practices prove absurd and grotesque, they will have to be modified or dropped. It is impossible to understand why otherwise right-thinking people should insist on perpetuating fashions that would shock even the less intelligent people elsewhere, who may not know what the fashion is in their own locality but see it as absurd to live in the two obviously different worlds depicted by shirt or jacket worn on top of African pants or loincloth—the more so in an age when movies available in most capitals of the world illustrate what would appear more appropriate.

For Africans anywhere to persist in this puppet dress must be regarded as perverted conservatism, which in any case is neither deep nor genuine enough. It cries out for a change. No effort will be made here to discuss which is the "right" or "wrong" or "better" of the various combinations of African style with more universally accepted style.

WIGS: AN AFFRONT TO THE AFRICAN PERSONALITY

The hallmark of beauty can be defined as that which remains serene, genuine, and as natural and as untouched as possible. It is *raw* beauty. This beauty first makes itself manifest at about the age of puberty, builds up steadily, and after the age of about twenty-five, it begins its slow decline, albeit with increasing grace and respect: the double chin; the unwanted hairs; the decaying teeth—some painful, some crippling; the wrinkled skin; the bald patches on the head—some seemingly reflecting erudition, others telling of misery and hardship; the graying hair—on the head, on the face, on the chest and everywhere; the lumps, the bumps; and fat all over—or skin thinly layered on the dry, aching bones.

Indeed, old age has matured to become one of the most bizarre problems of our time—how to cope with it, how to defeat it, how to live in it. Old age is intriguing to man, even more intriguing than death itself is. It is the newest epidemic on earth. No one likes old age; no one likes its insults and ravages. Everyone wants to defeat it, if only by a couple of years. Yet it comes. And it wins. In the midst of it all, we believe we must enter into our graves with as much youth as possible—with all our teeth intact, all organs intact and never under the radicalism of the surgeon, no added spare parts, no scars, no dentures, no wigs. We must return just as we came. It remains one of his frailties and vanities, perhaps pardonable, for man, whatever his station or his class, to attempt to remain perpetually beautiful and young. After all, he is an image of God.

Far and away the most serious, the most ominous and perhaps the most controversial crisis that has hit (and is hitting very hard indeed) the African personality in this generation is the increasingly popular fashion of wearing wigs.

Admittedly the indication for wigs may have become stronger as life expectancy has in recent decades been lengthened by thirty years or so.

To the African of this generation the problems posed by aging have even deeper meanings in a more sophisticated world and with incredible propinquity with the rest of mankind. The African in Europe and Asia is a rare bird enough, but the aging African is rarer still. At home he must appear like those younger ones—with all the unprecedented fashions. Should the hair be plaited, straightened, curled, pruned or shaven? And where? Should it be dyed, and if so to what color or colors? Should age be allowed to show, to tell? The head must be kept apparently uncovered; hair must show, if only in fringes—dye cannot be enough. The metamorphosis is the wig—jet-black, definite, straight, international and interracial—nothing like it ever before—what magic! what unbelievable and delightful rejuvenation!

The essential difference between, on the one hand, plastic surgery and cosmetics for enhancing beauty—erasing scars, adjusting lumps and bumps, bleaching and smoothening the skin—and the wearing of wigs on the other is that the latter is not additive but substitutive, it is not combative but evasive, it obscures and transforms, at times violently and recklessly. It would often amount to a flagrant betrayal of race and a travesty of natural beauty in the race concerned, the more so when it belongs to some other race with whom the wearer is in close contact. Yet it remains an open fact that most women would shudder to see some other woman appear in the same dress with them, unannounced, at any function, or even at ordinary times. To them it is most embarrassing—their originality smashed, their fire, their thunder, all stolen! Therefore, in interracial relations, the thin, long, straight hair uncharacteristic of the African would only serve to accentuate any pre-existing disregard of the African as a personality.

At sight, the essential part of any person is his head. Without his head he simply cannot be given any identity, much less be remembered. The head is a great determinant of beauty and of personality. The head is the temple of the body, and it should be kept sacred and held high. To have anything whatever to hide on the head must be accepted as a misfortune. The head can be adorned, but only in so far as it will command and attract even greater reverence, not suspicion. What, after all, remains of personal grace and beauty when over half the head (and perhaps the whole of the nape of the neck) is masqueraded?—a subjective, hidden entity.

Since the hair, in color, texture, density, shape, length, style, can be so effective in giving an identity to the head and in transforming the head and indeed the entire personality, to substitute (a wig) for the hair itself, rather than actually adorning the whole head or adorning one's natural hair, is the first step to losing one's personality, and losing it in a way which is cheap—cheap in the sense that just anyone who can afford it can be similarly transformed.

If wigs were hats, then their ridiculous nature would not be brought home immediately; no one would have any grave doubts about their probity. But wigs are deliberately meant to create a false impression that they are one's own genuine and natural hair; at least, they can often give others this impression (which, all the same, is a false but a beautifying one). Hats, on the other hand, would not give the impression that they are part and parcel of one's God-given beauty; rather, hats usually stand out as extraneous adornments which can be changed and which can be removed at will and in public.

It is in interracial relations that the wearing of wigs by Africans attains its extraordinary distasteful absurdity, reducing the whole of human natural beauty and grace to a mere gimmick. The person of African descent wearing the long straight "human" (or animal) hair or wearing nylon or some other material fashioned to imitate a type of hair that differs generally from that of his own race has obviously capitulated and inwardly admitted that he is not the true picture of what he expects the beautiful human to be or that he is not the best specimen of the natural beauty to be found in his own race. He is not as beautiful as he wants to be. He looks rather ugly to himself. He does not like his own looks. He would like to see himself transformed into something outwardly better than, or different from, what he actually knows himself to be.

At best, wigs may be permissible when they are used to cover an embarrassing baldness and will be recognized as performing only such a function. Otherwise, the fashion of wearing wigs destroys human physical and spiritual values, it vulgarizes and demeans human beauty as something terribly artificial which money can always buy—and the more money you put into it, the better the effect you get out of it.

Wigs as extraneous adornments are far more objectionable than dentures. Whereas the toothless individual is often shy about giving a broad smile, the wig wearer dons the wig purposefully for display and in an attempt to deceive and cajole everyone—but himself.

The wig often appears to take something away from one's scrupulousness and integrity and add an air of rascality or nonchalance to the personality. At other times the wig appears merely as a huge joke, not meant to be taken seriously by anyone. It betrays a desperate determination to appear handsome and unmarked. It remains one of the most unfortunate and disgusting popular fashions of our generation. Here indeed is incontrovertible evidence of a lack of self-confidence in one's own natural beauty, or in one's own racial beauty as a group.

Indeed, the wearing of European and Asiatic hairs by Africans is a sickening effort and an undisguised betrayal of the African personality. In a forthright way it epitomizes the capitulation of the African to non-African influences.

Again, African professionals who wear wigs patterned to appear like the natural long, straight hair of the Europeans of earlier centuries have little or nothing to justify a practice which is unwarranted, unbecoming, farfetched and clownish and which cries lustily for a change.

THE FADING AFRICAN LANGUAGES

One of the distinctive characteristics of man in the animal kingdom is his language and, more pointedly, the ability to formulate and comprehend the written word.

African languages are among the last citadels of African culture which have not completely succumbed to foreign in-

fluences. These languages are about the only thing on which the
African can still claim to be the absolute and unassailable
authority. African languages, especially African names, are a
source of invaluable pride to many Africans of this age. These
languages are unique, original and intensely African.

Language is an essential and powerful instrument of diplomacy. The visiting head of government insists on speaking the
official language of his own country, not necessarily out of pride
—for he may, in fact, be a great exponent of the host country's
language—but because, all in all, force or fuss must be met with
equal force or fuss.

It would greatly enhance the African personality if it were
able to address world organizations in its own native tongue.
But this is never the case, nor is there any hope now or ever that
it can be completely achieved even if it were allowed. Already
the languages of Europe dominate science, technology, economics and other disciplines. It is inconceivable that words from
these languages will not be introduced, indispensably, into the
indigenous languages of Africa and Asia. Most of these words are
often coined by unknown great men who hide in the corners of
laboratories all over Europe and North America. In the mid-
fifties the Indians found themselves short of thousands of Hindi
words to match scientific, technological and socio-economic
development. The same will certainly obtain with any of the
most popular African languages.

Languages change all the time. That is probably the process
that keeps them alive and vigorous. Today the languages of
Africa are not confronted with change for the sake of vigor.
They are confronted with change tending to certain extinction
from the human wealth of languages.

The African in possession of at least one of the languages of
the continent considers himself especially fortunate when he goes
abroad; it gives a shot in the arm to his personality. No one
thanks him for his expertise and experience in any non-African
language, the less so when it is known that he cannot speak the
one which should more naturally belong to him.

The first major psychological defeat for any African in the

comity of nations is that he has to borrow another tongue in order to speak for himself. Strangers to a language do often take more time over grammar and are in perpetual thirst for vocabulary and at times phonetics. Be that as it may, the advantages conferred are at least limited by the fact that one has been forced to play an "away match" and would necessarily train harder for it. To the African in particular, one cannot expect it to be "natural" for him to speak a European language as a matter of routine, at home or even abroad. It is even more difficult for him to go into the rather unpleasant explanation of how he came to pick it up.

These most influential European languages today dominate all the phenomenal transformations taking place everywhere in the world. They enjoy a predominance even over Chinese, which is spoken by over one-sixth of the world's population. Greek and Latin once prevailed, but today they count for naught in most places, even in Europe. Nevertheless, one finds the indelible imprints of Latin in those parts of Europe which were once within the Holy Roman Empire.

It will be difficult to erase English and French from the face of Africa, especially because of their international tender and because of the excessive desire and need for economic and industrial development in Africa.

The African or the Asiatic can well become a professor of one of the European languages in his own country or even abroad. His selection may be deserving in every way, divorced from nationalistic sentiments. But can he ever become an authority in the language? It will matter little if he started learning from the cradle. It is not quite natural to accept him as an authority; he simply is not a natural custodian of the language. The same of course goes for strangers to certain African or Asiatic languages.

Certain non-Africans have often commended the literary efforts of African poets, playwrights and novelists. At the same time they have expressed the candid and considered opinion that these Africans would probably be better employed writing in or translating into their own tongues. But the African writer may want to make his brillance and impact felt on the international scene. He is unlikely to achieve this by appealing to an audience of less than ten million, nor has he in fact the training to do this as effectively as he already can do it in certain European languages. He must first get to Europe before he can express, to the best of his ability, what is essentially African. In the end he will be unable, dumbfounded, to express what is African as an African should. As far as language is concerned, the African, renascent and resurgent, swims uphill in a sea of dilemma.

African languages are often said to number in the hundreds. But leading authorities are now convinced that the languages of Africa derive from only four families. Excluding the Malayo-Polynesian languages, which are spoken in Madagascar, it is said that there are four main language families: first, the Niger-Congo group, which includes Bantu, Fulani, Mende and Swahili; second, the Nilo-Saharan group, which extends across the area between the Niger and the Nile; third, the Afro-Asiatic group, which includes Semitic (Arab and Hebrew), ancient Egyptian, Berber and Hausa; fourth, the Khoisan languages, which dominate parts of Southern Africa.

European languages are used officially in all African countries. National languages are used in Tanzania (Swahili), the Somali Republic (Somali) and Mauritania (Arabic), but even in these areas English is the official and predominant language.

In general each tribe or nation possesses one language, and each of these languages has various dialects.

Without disputing the validity or family relations of the languages in Africa, the point of particular interest is whether and for how long the languages spoken by the indigenous peoples today are going to last. Are they going to be swept aside in favor of the European languages—English, French, Portuguese and Spanish—which have been introduced into the continent only within the last two centuries?

Most of these African languages are spoken by fewer than five million people. The two most popular ones are Hausa in West Africa and Swahili in East and Southern Africa.

To decry the English or the French language in Africa is to decry science and technology and close all ears and eyes to the rest of the world. These languages are the lingua franca; in fact, they form part of the cement that binds the various ethnic groups that constitute these new nations. They are therefore at the moment indispensable. Yet if these languages of international currency are allowed to completely eclipse the local languages, all African languages are likely to be lost and perhaps forever; the last stronghold of African spiritual heritage will have crumbled, and the African will forever remain unoriginal, unauthoritative and unauthentic about any literary work. Posterity will be forever dispossessed. All that will be left are African names, whose meanings, today still greatly cherished, will steadily get blurred as generations succeed generations in their neglect.

Parochial arrogance and an unbridled quest for the European way of life demand that those who speak the smaller languages should prefer to learn English or French to learning any of the bigger languages in their own countries, which to them is a waste of time. They would prefer to jump into the international scene straightaway: it is more realistic, more profitable and more durable. As things stand it will be rather too optimistic to hope that the smaller languages can last up to the end of the present century.

Are African countries merely hoping against hope in their attempt to salvage their languages on the one hand, while on the other they nurse an inordinate desire for Western education and for science, technology and socio-economic advancement in their territories? Can an African language or two be developed and seasoned to meet the challenge of rapid socio-economic development?

The future of these languages is at best bleak. Already in Nigeria, for example, most educated people encourage their children to speak English and then enter schools which place great emphasis on English and often teach none of the Nigerian languages. The hope is that these children will pick up the local language anyway in the neighborhood. But these environments are getting steadily barren. Again, in Nigeria, as in other areas of Africa, Greek and Latin are accredited for a university degree. These old European languages can also be subjects for higher qualifications. But only few of the indigenous languages are taught in secondary schools, much less in universities, and lesser still are the prospects of establishing Chairs in these local languages. The study of Greek and Latin in Africa may have been one of the truly good things of colonialism, but it must be considered elegant and too luxurious in the new era in which Africa can undoubtedly manage very well with only English or French and if possible Russian or Chinese.

Greek and Latin are in fact gradually receding into oblivion in many European and American universities. They no longer command the pride of place accorded to them in medieval times and even until recent decades. Therefore in Africa where there is a pathetic shortage of students in science, agriculture, economics, engineering, medicine, etcetera, there is little justification for spending public money on the study of what must be unimportant and irrelevant anachronisms in this age of science, and even of culture.

African languages must not be allowed to fade away. They must be nourished and nurtured by this generation on whom so very much depends, for the use and wholesomeness of posterity. If the opportunity is not seized immediately, it will never be retrieved.

It should be possible to teach at least two languages in every school in Africa—a local one and a national one.

English and French are the official languages of the O.A.U. But cannot a continental language be agreed upon—a language which is truly African? Swahili and Hausa both spring to mind. Surely the African is not being oversentimental or ridiculous in adopting a native language which has the potential of becoming the official language throughout the continent.

It is embarrassing enough that Africans of the same "nationality" but of different "tribes" should have to converse in a language which is totally out of their own world. It becomes even more significant, lamentable and ominous when Africans of different nationalities but of the same tribe are unable to comprehend one another at all, even in their own indigenous tribal language, yet are able to speak English or French quite fluently. This is reminiscent of the passengers who have to fly to London, then to Paris, then back to Africa in order to travel between the two capitals on the west coast! These are colonial landmarks which are being erased.

There are some Africans who in their illiteracy and frivolity demean European languages and grammars. These corrupted European languages are often called pigeon or coastal. They may sound funny and even ingenious, but they only have a demoralizing and confusing effect on the standard of English and French as spoken or written internationally. To cater to popular demand, advertisements are occasionally carried on the air and on the screen in these peculiar versions of English or French. This undoubtedly introduces a new nausea into the African world of make-believe.

There can be no doubt whatever that language has a central role in creating a sense of oneness in each African country and in fact throughout the continent. Marriages between peoples from different linguistic groups will be more widespread, and mutual understanding will be enhanced.

The fewer languages, the more economical and efficient will be national or continental methods of mass communication.

There are obvious difficulties. There is the usual conservatism in each area. No one likes his own tribe or language to be subordinated to any other. This is purely a political problem. The world knows about the perennial strife in Belgium, Ceylon and elsewhere. A great deal of statesmanship will be needed everywhere in the endeavor to create national languages. A continental language sponsored by the O.A.U. would probably be a more acceptable language than one which could seriously aggravate tribalism or even split a country.

The fact that certain languages in the British Isles have given their own lives for the promotion of the English language would probably appease tribalism in Africa. Nevertheless, it will be best to promote and perpetuate each and every language everywhere in Africa, not for the sake of tribalism or academics but for the sake of culture. The African in the international scene needs as much as possible of what is left of African culture. To deliberately allow any language to disappear by not teaching it in local schools or by not according it official recognition would be robbing Africa as a whole of one of the spokes in the wheel of her cultural heritage.

AFRICAN SCRIPTS

In old African universities writing took the form of Arabic. No one can say exactly when the first attempts to evolve truly indigenous African scripts were made. It is common knowledge, however, that the Vai people of Liberia had theirs; in 1815 there was an exhibition of Vai script in England.

The Bamoun script in the Cameroons and the Nsibidi and Toma scripts are among other well-known African scripts. Moreover, here and there, in many parts of the continent, inscriptions are found which are meaningless to anyone of the present generation but most probably meant something to whoever made them.

Roman script came into Africa as part and parcel of Europeanism, and many editions of the Holy Bible in African languages are written in Roman script.

It is very doubtful indeed whether anything can be gained by either attempting to revive any old African scripts or even writing a new one entirely. One fact nevertheless remains: No one can ever know how far to go now, and what exactly can be done by the present generation in their conscious attempt to book a front seat for Africans of subsequent generations in relation to other peoples. What may sound madly ridiculous or impossible today may well turn out to be a definite asset in many ways for generations yet unborn. This particularly applies to several aspects of culture.

In a world of so many peoples, whatever aspect of cultural heritage predominates represents a triumph for will power and possibly with unknown and unlimited advantage therefrom.

THE CRISIS OF IDENTITY

The multitude of tongues in each African country has been a source of confusion as regards personal identities. While some people prefer to be addressed as Mr. or M., according to which European language is officially used in their countries, others take their own indigenous equivalent translation of these titles. No attempt will be made here to give a list of the scores of popular ones. Suffice it to note that they represent a protest, often personal, at being normally mistaken for the European.

In African forums, and in world assemblies, Africans from independent countries are still addressed according to which country once ruled them. This does not do credit to the solidarity that should exist among the representatives of the continent; it only serves to perpetuate the imperial lines that had rigidly divided them.

Feelings similar to these must also be engendered in the outside world—a thing that cannot be said to conform, in all catholicity, with the policy of positive neutrality which most independent African countries claim to be pursuing.

To look for a continental title would be just as difficult as to foist one language on the whole continent.

The inherent desire of the individual African to be first and foremost African by name had always been expressed everywhere on the continent. The early European Christian encouraged Africans to adopt biblical names. Ordinary European Christian names soon became commonplace. Depending upon which was the colonial master, one found, for example, Andrew, André, Andreas or Andres; or or Alfred, Alfret or Alfredo. Soon everyone began to appreciate that indigenous names could be valid as names in the Christian church. It is increasingly uncommon to use biblical names in some African Christian churches.

Indigenous African religions believe in the same Almighty God as is taught by the Bible. Christian (first) names given to children are almost always meaningful. Often they amount to a prayer or a thanksgiving, or they relate the circumstances of the family at the period of birth of the new baby. At other times they describe the nature of the pregnancy or of the delivery, such as twin or breech.

Again, here the Muslim religion has stood conspicuously apart. Muslims bear names related to their own religion and have never displayed fascination for European names to the extent of adopting them. The general trend everywhere is to derive names from the local languages.

There are other manifestations of the African's silent and assiduous attempt to give himself an image. Certain political leaders simply adopt a local title for *leader,* such as "chief," or assume well-known honorary titles such as the British knighthood which allowed the outstanding African, usually elected and recommended by the local British authority to belong to certain noble orders in the British Isles. (There has never been an African or Asiatic British lord, though a few leaders, even after their checkered history as political agitators, became "privy councillors.") Others call themselves doctors on account of honorary doctorate degrees conferred on them by foreign universities, even when they never went to any school, much less to a university.

Sometimes African tradition and European language come into open clash. *Chief* is not an African word, yet the most ardent traditionalists would prefer this to any local translation. The chieftaincy title itself is totally eclipsed by the individual's own surname: the title appears to have been accepted not so much with dedication to the noble ideals of the chieftaincy institution which needs perpetuating as for personal aggrandizement in which the new chief can bask. The African could well borrow a leaf from the British noble who would dismiss his surname to perpetuate a hereditary title in salute of his noble ancestors and their institutions which must flourish.

Members of a parliament often answer to *Honourable* instead of passing as the equivalent of Mr.

The most obvious examples of changes in name that have occurred include Ghana, Mali, Malawi, Zambia, Lesotho, Botswana and Kinshasa, all of which threw overboard the baptismal names accorded them by Europe. In every country, institutions, cities and streets have been renamed to keep up with the legitimate aspirations of the new era. These are commendable and practical ways of re-establishing African local languages and identities. It must at the same time be quite an unpleasant thing that persons who did certain types of pioneering work in Africa cannot be commemorated by leaving their names as they stood under colonial rule. Africa has got to protect her culture and create an atmosphere that will not embarrass anyone.

It is quite striking that none of the early explorers of Africa, like Mungo Park, the Landers, Bath and Clapperton, have anything substantial to commemorate them. Quite often it seems even more embarrassing to the European than it does to the African that certain vestiges of colonialism should still remain years after political independence was granted—for example, X City, Yville.

The Morality of the Poverty Line

It is relevant to consider here, in connection with the African personality, certain aspects of public life in African countries which can be of profoundest significance in the over-all socio-economic development of the continent.

Bribery and corruption are said to be quite common in independent Africa. This impression is widespread in the far-advanced countries which are rendering considerable help in the fight against disease, hunger, poverty and misery in Africa.

Books have been written to describe, with incontrovertible evidence, how corruption is practiced in certain African countries, at times in the highest places in public life.

In Europe and North America, parliamentarians and the general public have begun to be quite skeptical about offering their hard-won resources to aid the peoples of Africa, simply because they are not always sure that these aids would reach their desired target, the ordinary man in the street. Moreover, a lot of criticism is occasionally leveled in these far-advanced countries at the alarming extravagance of prestigious and unnecessary projects in a number of African countries.

Bribery and corruption in official circles was certainly confirmed in certain African countries in the earlier years of independence by commissions of inquiry. Extravagance and prestigious projects, however, are subjective entities. Various countries would justify their expenditures and plans as being parts of their national aspiration.

The European or American taxpayer may not very well understand how the African in public life has been able to amass enormous personal wealth within the last decade, but he may understand that some of these governments are quite ambitious, and that even if they seem to be putting the cart before the horse, this is a function of the prevailing sense of priority, not necessarily of corruption.

The Taj Mahal, St. Peter's Cathedral, the Eiffel Tower and St. Paul's Cathedral may possibly have matched their own world, their own circumstances and their own times, but the world is now much smaller. There is greater international cooperation than in previous centuries. Extravagance, whether in the pursuit of peace, war, science or national fulfillment, anywhere, has become the concern of the whole of humanity. Yet it remains the inalienable right of each sovereign country to decide what is extravagant and what is not, what the country can afford and what it cannot.

National monuments costing millions of pounds which even the far-advanced countries themselves can ill afford for a similar purpose are unlikely to go very well anywhere for a country which has to live on the dole, knocking, cap in hand, from door to door to collect moneys and investments for improving the lot of its citizens of this generation.

Bribery and corruption in African countries can be divided into two kinds: that which occurs among the citizens of the country and that which involves foreigners. The two are equally abominable. The international type can be regarded as a universal practice. In desperate Africa, beset with such incredible poverty in the midst of such incredible potentialities, international bribery must readily pass as treason. Any type of national betrayal for the sake of personal wealth must invariably be dealt with ruthlessly and in the severest terms possible.

Are there certain factors which make the average African more susceptible to bribery, corruption and nepotism than his counterpart in Europe, America or Asia? Are these related to the customs and other socio-psychological factors in the African background?

All the evils and goodnesses of which man is capable are best unveiled by his personal circumstances. Sense of humor and transient emotional reactions may vary from race to race and with ethnic groups. But no convincing evidence has ever been advanced to suggest that certain groups are innately more or less belligerent, criminal, violent or lazy than others or that they are more or less humorous, emotional, generous, kind or honest. Indeed, no scientific data leading to these conclusions can ever be acceptable until due consideration has been given to the *leadership* of the people, to the prevailing sense of values of the people and to preconditioning factors, such as history, wealth, poverty, group loyalties and foreign influences, which can substantially influence the day-to-day life of the people concerned.

Most people are human enough to be greatly tempted to seize an advantage whenever that advantage is worth it. The African who has lived among Europeans, Asiatics or Americans soon gets to appreciate that every society, however advanced or religious, has its own share of criminals, its own share of psychopaths and other unfortunate elements.

In the far-advanced countries, banks and wealthy homes can be robbed in such an incredibly well organized manner that when one comes to read about the robberies, credit, rather than curse, would almost go to the robbers for their brilliance and expertise. On the other hand, the African must be very impressed with the fact that the tendency to cheat others, to exploit the ignorance of others, to accept bribes, to profiteer, even though this is found in the far-advanced countries, is very rare indeed compared with what obtains in his own country. When, however, these practices do occur in the far-advanced countries, they usually involve substantial moneys, perhaps thousands or millions of pounds, and there are detective networks specially trained to track such criminals, not to mention spies and international traitors.

Again, in the far-advanced countries people in public life have to maintain transparent honesty. They must be wide-awake to public opinion. They must never betray the public trust. *Noblesse oblige* is the watchword.

Furthermore, the law protects everyone, and the average citizen understands his fundamental human rights and would exercise such rights through parliamentarians, lawyers, the press, the trade unions and various humanitarian pressure groups.

The press often constitutes a sensitive invigilator and would expose anyone who falls short of the very high standards demanded of him by society. It is not ridiculous to add that not only are even helpless children protected by voluntary organizations, but there are also those organizations that strive to protect various needy members of the society and would even protect animals. All these have grown with centuries of trial, error and experience.

The African situation is sharply different in a variety of ways. Most people are still abjectly poor; financial security is the exception.

The temptation to cheat, lie and commit such apparently mean degrees of crime as stealing a hen or breaking into a house can be so overwhelming as to arouse pity, and deserve understanding and forgiveness. This cannot be correlated with shoplifting, which is a universal practice and may have a different reason, perhaps a psychological one, motivating it.

Profiteering and exploitation of members of the community in various ways are quite common in developing countries. Others resort to begging and pretend to be incapable of any form of manual labor. All these are reflections of the prevalent poverty; they are not necessarily reflections of immorality, nor are they reflections of godlessness or of contempt for the arm of the law. Undoubtedly the natives of far-advanced countries went through this stage of social evolution some decades or even years ago. In the richer countries, for example, one is unlikely to meet a shopkeeper who would take undue advantage of any foreigner because of language or ignorance. The simple reason: it is not worth it. After all, how much can the foreigner possibly spend for one to risk one's name or fortune? But if the amount involved is temptingly high, then another proposition entirely may arise.

Bribery and Corruption

Traditional African communal life is rich with various gestures of fellowship. Food is shared among all, and in places many people eat from the same plate. The distribution of kola nuts in certain areas is a sacred symbol of friendship and trust. Kola nuts are essentially akin to coffee and tea. They have not, unfortunately, invaded the international market as have tobacco, coffee and tea. Perhaps when kola nuts can get magnificently wrapped, and packed in golden pouches, they will become available to the whole world. Kola nuts have a ritual similar to the offering and lighting up of cigarettes—they are to be split open in a special way and shared by all. So far no one has been able to accuse kola nuts of being inimical to the human body.

It is never easy to know when a particular offer amounts to a bribe—whether within a family or between nations. A gift is usually offered as a symbol of friendship, but this may only be an ostensible reason. It may have been given in return for some other gift or as a reward for a past deed or simply to buy the recipient over, in a rather honorable and subtle way, in anticipation of some definite favor.

Tips are also given, not only voluntarily but at times officially in some of the far-advanced countries. In certain areas of Africa the "dash" is given as an open present for a favor just done or just about to be done.

In the colonial era, before the standard of living rose to the levels now found in Africa, brides and cows, goats, sheep, kola nuts, alcohol, tobacco, food and other "presents" were acceptable as bribes. Today the situation has changed tremendously; hard cash, and other means of bribery and corruption which can be found in the far-advanced countries, are about the only effective means of attracting favors.

But why should some of those who seem to be reasonably well remunerated in some African countries descend to taking bribes and joining in practices and negotiations which by all civilized standards must amount to contemptible pieces of fraud? Why should there be nepotism—the type which leaves any right-thinking person with no doubt at all that Peter has been callously robbed to pay Paul?

In the traditional way of life in most parts of Africa, and moreover as taught by Christianity, Islam and certain African indigenous religions, all members of the community must live in brotherly love, charity and honesty. It must never be enough for an individual to be well fed, sheltered and clothed, and psychologically and physically secure; he must ensure that all his immediate relations are adequately cared for. His circle of relations extends from his children to his distant cousins; parallel with these, his neighbors, and at times his neighbors' dependents, are also largely dependent on him. As a result the citizen whose actual income compares favorably with his professional colleague's in Western Europe may be saddled with financial responsibilities which are tenfold the latter's, the lower cost of living in Africa notwithstanding. Therefore, although he allegedly is well remunerated, the holes in his pockets are so many that he can neither save any money nor even adequately fulfill those responsibilities which, by tradition and by his own brand of sense of responsibility, belongs to him. He must nevertheless strive to make ends meet. This citizen, once he has achieved his not-so-enviable position, is in a way just as insecure financially as the simple poor man whose abject poverty is quite obvious to everyone and from whom society expects little or no material help.

This well-remunerated but poor man is exposed to as many temptations as can be found around him. He must help his son, or his cousin or his neighbor's son or his uncle, to get that vacant post or that house, that car, that landed property, at the best bargain possible. He must see to it that a nephew gets into some school and is awarded a local scholarship. He must help in ensuring that one business contract or another falls into the lap of one of his dependents. He cannot afford to let the side down; he faces not only pernicious gossip, pestering and embarrassing boycott but also the charge of being heartless and selfish for not helping while some other people allegedly are being helped. Vicious circle!

He must continue indefatigably to use all his influence, position, power and money and even his honor and his conscience everywhere, and at all times, not directly to benefit himself but mainly to ease his overburdened shoulders of some of the onerous and inescapable responsibilities thrust upon him through his own sense of belonging to a particular family, town, district, subethnic group, ethnic group, section of the country and then ultimately the country itself.

The citizen is repaid with the grateful, loyal support and hero worship accorded to him by his ethnic group, subethnic group, town or family in every aspect of his own personal aspiration. In fact, he may have attained his high position mainly through these varying degrees of sectional support to which he still owes much of his stability. As such this man is insecure in many ways without the buttresses he has built around himself or that have built themselves around him. Should he break the vicious circle in his own favor, on any account, he stands condemned and he will be virtually ostracized by these dependents. Then, similar forces of bribery and corruption and nepotism come face to face between individuals, families, subethnic groups and ethnic groups. It is not surprising, therefore, that sectionalism and tribalism inflame corruption in many parts of Africa.

As long as tribalism remains an appreciable influence in the public or political life of any country, nepotism will ever be a malignant instrument of injustice and oppression to individuals and groups.

Some of these young countries as a whole are underdeveloped. They are not yet convincingly, once and for all, established to the extent of driving the forces of tribalism and sectionalism underground. Everyone finds greater security in casting his lot with his tribe rather than with the nation. He sees little use in helping a member of another tribe before helping a member of his own. Rather, he would victimize a member of another tribe in order to consolidate his own insecure position within his own tribe. Not as in the far-advanced countries, where national moral standards tend to be discernible, in most African countries it is tribal moral standards that tend to be discernible, and to prevail over what may be regarded as national moral standards. National moral standards, decency and fair play can be imposed only by drastic measures applied by the central authority.

The New African Sense of Values

Family and ethnic responsibilities cannot alone explain the feeling of material insecurity often found among citizens with apparently adequate incomes in the developing countries. Greed and a peculiar sense of values, which at least is much less obvious among peoples in the far-advanced countries, form significant factors.

The background of the African may be involved. Although a great deal is often made of the prominent African citizen who began life in a rather hard way, walking miles to school sometimes very early in the morning, it must be remembered that no parent would have risked his child's life in any extraordinary manner. Other children underwent similar hardship—going to the farm or walking many miles to collect four gallons of water to be carried on the head.

However, could his inordinate urge to get rich still be due to an unexpected burst into a life of luxury and other hitherto undreamt-of opportunities which resulted from the departure of the colonial government? Must he appear overprosperous just because he knows he was once destitute? Must he ignore those still suffering because he is callous or because he wants them to show their own incentiveness and scale the slippery ladder as he himself did?

By far the most significant point is that some of the more prosperous Africans are victims of the terrible strains and temptations of being in too close contact with the much richer and prosperous life of Europe and North America. Some of them have lived in it, tasted of it, and have grown up within the context of Western prosperity and luxuries. The consequences of this can be very far-reaching.

The African who is considered locally to be a rich man is naturally eager to maintain this status. He is also aware, perhaps more than anyone else, that he is nowhere near the world's richest men, some of whom he has heard of, or even met somehow in Africa or elsewhere. In his journeys abroad he has seen a lot of what must be irresistibly desirable to possess.

Cruelly pitched against human weaknesses and human vanity are the abundances and joys of life. They are all without limit: relaxation—an endless pursuit, according to the individual; beautiful things—new ones quickly rendered archaic by yet more beautiful and ever more fashionable ones, more so in the age of technology: machines—toys, cars, helicopters, private airplanes; things that bring greater comforts and even greater joys; things that make life more convenient—an endless list; things that appeal just because they are a different variety; things that promise more and more personal security—socially, physically, mentally and economically; things that enhance personal pride— the best ever, in quality and quantity, under the sun. And to possess alone, to be seen, envied and acclaimed as the most successful of all times, and finally to ensure that all these are perpetuated in one's own name—these seem objectives worthy of energetic pursuit.

The desire to own an expensive sports car that will do 100 miles per hour on primitive African roads is understandable. Whether this desire can be fulfilled will depend on whether the car is allowed into the country or not. Thus the official attitude toward car ownership and the environmental attitude toward the possession of a car are relevant factors in deciding whether the car will be bought, or the money will be spent on something else.

The contemporary sense of values in many African countries is that the successful man must exhibit his wealth as an index of his success. Vanity is thus encouraged; accumulation of wealth and the exhibition of it for the world to see is the rule, not the exception. It matters little how the wealth was acquired, even when all one's sources of income are known to all and sundry. An environment such as this inevitably gives rise to a competitive spirit among the general population. The acquisition of wealth must proceed by every means possible. The citizen fears little from the now decadent, unprogressive and unrealistic social and religious ethics regarding, debt, overdraft, loans liquidation, etcetera. Instead, hire-purchase and other imported methods of getting things done, of living in advance of the future, must be copied; one must not be despicable by modern, present-day international standards.

Why would not one rather accept his own lot and abstain from this epidemic rat race? Society is young, life is still new to all, in emergent Africa. The successful man is still a novelty. He wants to be seen and admired and envied by neighbors, friends and relatives. No family and no individual would accept that they have been beaten. Everyone still believes he can prosper. He has seen his less talented colleagues rise to wealth or success overnight; he too could do the same if only he knew the secret.

In the far-advanced countries, direct taxation and indirect taxation are means of squeezing moneys out of the more fortunate members of the society for the benefit of all. In developing countries, however, it cannot be enough to rely on these measures. Taxes are always easy to evade in the thick fog of bribery and corruption, inefficiency and social insecurity. If the exhibition of wealth were prevented, it is clear that austerity rather than squandermania would be the rule and there would be more saving toward the capital so much needed in these countries.

Africa and World Charity

The African of this generation is universally regarded as a very poor man. Informed opinion is quite aware nevertheless that potentially this same African could be as rich as the average citizen of any other continent if the resources of the continent were fully tapped and equitably distributed in the legitimate interests of the peoples of Africa.

Africa receives foreign aid from several European and American countries. From Africa, delegation after delegation travels all over the world requesting loans, grants, investments, teachers, knowledge and so on. These are all aspects of the international cooperation of which no one is particularly ashamed. Indeed, only the United States, the Soviet Union and perhaps West Germany and China can do without foreign aid in one form or another. Most African countries express the desire not to allow these aids to jeopardize their political independence in any way. They emphasize their decision to remain neutral in the East-West cold war.

How do these foreign benevolences affect the African as a personality?

There are the scores of voluntary organizations in Europe and America which undertake international philanthropic work. In many instances moneys collected from the public in European and American cities run into thousands of pounds. In newspapers, handbills and posters, in television and the movies, in churches and schools, at bazaars and on the streets, lavish campaigns are embarked upon to collect alms from the general public in cities and towns of the European world for the poor, needy, starving and wretched masses in Africa (and other underdeveloped countries).

No one would question the kindly conscience that inspires these enterprises, which often entail a lot of energy, time, deliberation and other sacrifices. Nevertheless, these voluntary organizations, more often than not, in their missionary zeal to collect moneys paint the most desperate picture of life in Africa (or other places) and have arrogated to themselves the divine missionary right to rescue her from disease and human misery.

The sympathy, disgust, horror, charity and other feelings of every single person in the European world is aroused to uplift the African and other needy peoples from their most appalling life. The feeling of common humanity would normally commend the humanitarian content of these gestures inspired by a few volunteers. But there are grievous reservations.

The activities and especially the propaganda of these voluntary organizations tend to give a sense of piousness and gratification in the donor countries which inevitably tends to obscure the realities of history, of colonial exploitation, incompetence and suppression, and of current international economic relations. It is true that these organizations may also have been engaged in solving the crux of Africa's problems—attaining economic independence and acquiring foreign capital investment or loans. It is well known that if these were actually forthcoming, there would be such sudden socio-economic transformation of the continent that no one in Europe and America would need to be bothered and pestered any longer about the emaciated and suffering African.

Can one actually expect the European who began to throw his pennies into the boxes almost from the cradle, then gave his silver at school, and then in his adult life gave his gold, through taxes and voluntary donations and the rescue operations in Africa, to deeply regard the African personality as anything better than his burden? Even though self-imposed? The European child invariably grows up with the belief that the African cannot imagine how much he owes his very life to his personal charity and humanitarianism.

This is a root cause of racial or national arrogance which has emerged from quite untenable premises. This European citizen does not know how much he owes his current prosperity to the African continent and its people.

It can be argued that the African is in any case so abjectly poor and desperate that he has no choice between what his government, with all its proclaimed plans, can do for him and what some foreign organizations can do for him. For a recipient country to allow aids not channeled strictly between governments or between government agencies is the first admission of a degree of inability to cope with its most pressing problems. The image and honor of the country must be protected in the first place, especially if one cares to relate the moneys to how they are collected in the donor countries, albeit with a generous and sympathetic heart.

For the purpose of socio-economic development of African countries, all aids, loans and capitals are best arranged intergovernmentally.

What should be the attitude toward a million-pound offer, in gift or loan, first, from an individual person or an individual organization of any foreign country; second, from a foreign national government; and third, from private donations collected publicly from door to door and in the streets of another nation?

Undoubtedly the honor of the recipient country is affected in three different degrees. The most respectable offer must be the purely intergovernmental one. Here the beggar must be an honorable and purposeful beggar. If the foreign government does not think it fit to render help in the particular instance, then it is safe to assume that the consensus in that country does not consider the need great or urgent enough. The recipient country should do better without such help.

On the other hand natural disasters and unexpected tragedies are an extraordinary problem. They are of a different nature from chronic poverty or perennial agricultural or famine problems. National calamities need no appeal to common humanity before offers arrive spontaneously from anyone, of any group anywhere, and in any quantity, however meager. Such offers would always be received with grateful thanks by friends in desperate need from friends indeed.

A worthy and responsible government must be prepared to accept full responsibility for *all* national problems, especially when these are chronic. That is why it has been called upon to govern.

Can economic aid be compared with military aid? Suppose there are voluntary private armies in certain non-African countries which are prepared to help an African country in case it is attacked from outside or whenever a *coup d'état* attempt is being made. Would such offers be acceptable to any African country?

Beggary is commonplace in many parts of Africa. Beggary reflects the prevalent poverty and unemployment. It also reflects governmental and public standards and their principles regarding human dignity. It is part and parcel of poverty and unemployment. It should never be condoned by a responsible government nor by a responsible society. Some beggars are simply lazy and would often pretend to be incapable of any physical work on account of one deformity or another. Such are no longer allowed in the more civilized countries of Europe, where beggars are licensed after proven disabilities. Then they are still obliged to attract attention and justification by undertaking some responsibility that will interest society—playing some musical instrument, painting, and the like.

It must be ridiculous for private African organizations to go abroad to Europe or America to appeal for funds at public meetings to build roads, hospitals and other social amenities for their towns or tribes. At best such efforts are liable to all sorts of complications. Africa as a focus of humanitarian activity is the exact antithesis of Africa with will power and self-respect.

Unless African countries make determined efforts not to advertise their poverty, ludicrous international beggary will further expose the African personality to universal contempt. Africans probably merit no greater access or right to European or North American charity than the peoples of Spain, Portugal, Greece, southern Italy and South America.

Under the Spell of European Heroes

In most African countries the majority of the films shown in the theater and on television are neither African in origin nor African in cast. The reasons are to be found partly in the underdevelopment of the continent—underdevelopment not in the sense that there are not enough indigenous African plays, literature and music and the talent to promote them, but in the sense that Africa has not developed the requisite economic educational and technical resources to meet the standards already set in Europe and North America.

The educative and entertainment values of these media of mass communication are obvious. There is no doubt that African countries must feel a sense of great indebtedness to those European, North American and Asiatic countries that kindly and with all good intentions send, sell or lend their films and encourage the growth of these media in Africa, especially through international cultural agreements and through such world organizations as UNESCO.

Since independence many African countries have signed cultural agreements with the more powerful countries of Europe, America and Asia. In practice however, these cultural agreements are always terribly one-sided. The result is that movie and television shows of these foreign countries monopolize the screens of Africa for the better part of any evening or month. African shows seldom if ever find their way to screens outside the continent.

Moreover, the films from Africa are often shot or directed by foreigners. They are those that will satisfy popular demand abroad, usually by portraying the primitiveness in Africa or the landscape and fauna. By contrast, the films from Europe, America and Asia are of a wide variety that range from fiction to documentaries. They depict crime, glamour, luxury, violence, science and technology, and ordinary life in the areas of strong European or Asiatic influence.

The same is true as regards radio broadcasts and also the establishment of cultural centers.

What is the psychological impact on the African mind of these exceedingly effective media of mass communication and the material they carry?

The influence of foreign films imported into Africa is of the profoundest importance. As they are usually attractive, most

Africans rush to glue themselves to their foreign imageries and are carried away into a world to which essentially they do not belong, all in the name of entertainment.

To have an insight into what goes on in other lands is a good thing, but to be absorbed away into another land may be worse than not gaining an insight into that life at all.

These imported films are of course, more often than not, fictitious. They are gigantic fabrications and photo tricks elaborated by science and technology, rather than products of native ingenuity or the dexterity of the superb actors and actresses concerned.

The over-all effect is for the African to be led, consciously or subconsciously, to imitate and to endlessly admire and hero-worship these foreign actors and actresses. They can watch their hero and heroines on the screen hour in, hour out, night in, night out, whether in Europe or America or back home in Africa.

Local talents, having developed within the compass of this school, have to ascend its ladder to greatness—singing, dancing, acting and playing as what they are not, and in contexts which to them must be abstruse. Local fans follow suit. The end result is to attribute anything superlative—positively or negatively—to peoples outside their own world, far away in America, Asia and Europe. To be with it means to be without.

Again, it cannot necessarily be a reflection of poor quality nor can it be mere accident that even when the far-advanced countries have the World Service Radio broadcasts, they seldom if ever find it possible to transmit scores of plays, songs and music in other languages or about other foreign places to the rest of the world.

Are broadcasts outside one's shores really meant for the benefit of one's citizens sojourning elsewhere? Are they meant for the benefit of all mankind? Or are they a bombastic psychological cold war directed at the poorer countries, which are helplessly and permanently on the receiving end?

On the whole, a great deal can and must be said to commend European, American, Asiatic and other countries which sent their entertainment into Africa with all good intentions. Moreover, a great deal can still be done to promote international and inter-racial good will through cultural intercourse, as in the instances of UNESCO, national festivals and Commonwealth festivals. Nevertheless, it is of supreme importance to note the international and interracial psychology inherent in these proceedings. It is probably better not to be educated or entertained at all than to be educated and entertained in a way which in the final analysis will prove inimical to the proper growth of people and to their intrinsic dignity and wealth.

Conclusion

Whereas political independence was achieved in Africa through the spontaneous collective effort of the leaders and the people in each country, this cannot be the case with cultural emancipation.

Some of the issues raised in this chapter under "African Assertions" are exquisitely personal. They depend very much on the judgment, tastes, sense of values, experience and aspirations of each individual. The individual African is involved primarily as a person and secondarily as a member of an ethnic group or as a citizen of a country or as a continental citizen or as a world citizen. Moreover the individual is involved according to his religion, his profession and all other things dear to his heart.

Whereas the African in his native land, like the European in his, seldom bothers to think deeply about who he is and what he really stands for, the African who finds himself in a foreign country is quite often roused to do so. One supposes that the European or the Asiatic who finds himself in the minority anywhere is similarly affected.

The African's inner mental self is a strong force. Whatever he thinks or takes himself to be will affect his reaction to the various matters that may challenge his ego. The resilience of this inner mental self is greater than whatever anyone else may take him for.

What can the African think of himself, especially when he is driven by certain circumstances, and outside the African environment, to do so? As a member of a race, hardly anyone has endured as much as he has, nor can he imagine anything much worse. He belongs to a race which once was thoroughly humiliated, persecuted, exploited, dehumanized and brainwashed, until it lost faith in itself. Has this experience toughened or softened him, amused or angered him, spoiled or challenged him, rendered him hopeless or hopeful in the status quo?

Undoubtedly many Africans consider their lot on this earth already utterly hopeless. They are of the opinion that Africa can only continue to trail behind other continents as (they believe) it has always done. Some may have arrived at this conclusion after careful consideration of history and other evidences they have at their disposal. To others it is just a feeling that things cannot change, just because they appear unchangeable.

There are also those Africans who believe that, given certain circumstances, there is every conceivable chance that Africans can overtake all other continents not only in science and technology but also in re-establishing certain aspects of African culture, such as languages. It is also this group of Africans who appreciate how much is being lost every day by not marching forward as one continent with one destiny and under one leader.

It is quite possible to brainwash anyone and give him a magnified or a diminished sense of his importance. But then, not all the elements in a normal human being can be sunk at the same time. As long as the person remains, not in solitary confinement but in contact with other beings, and possesses all his senses, he will occasionally manage to see some good in himself. He only needs one single triumph over any other person to be reassured that he still has some potentialities and that if given a chance he can prove his mettle. The reverse is true as regards whoever has a magnified sense of his own importance: he need falter only once to realize that the fiction cannot be maintained or that it can be maintained only as relatively empty boasting.

African dialogue with Europe has been going on for the past four centuries and it has been quite bitter. Yet the world has witnessed similar events in other places, and it still is doing so.

Only a shallow African mind would bother to cry over the milk spilled centuries ago. Nevertheless, the past remains important if only for understanding the present and for being able to tackle it; it is also important in trying to prepare for the future. To the African the future matters even more than does the present.

The deep-thinking African realizes that slavery and colonialism has been the rule ever since the dawn of history; even the world's present greatest power was within recent centuries a colony, to a power which itself was a Roman colony. Yet how many people would call themselves Romans in this generation?

The crux of the problem as regards preparing for the future is to sweep aside as much of the relics of the shameful era as possible and to review, redefine and reconstruct the materialism and reincarnate the soul of the African continent.

The African needs mental emancipation. He must be allowed to drink deep of the waters of the history of old Africa; to convert the four centuries of European domination from an era of sheer waste and humiliation to one in which the foundations of a grander African tomorrow were laid and the fees for Western education duly paid. Now that it is over, as many vestiges of foreign culture and influence as possible must be steadily eliminated, at times drastically, but never with bitterness or oversentimentalism. The African henceforth must continue to evolve in his own way, within the context of his cultural heritage, his environment and the resources and resourcefulness of his continent.

He must feel maximally secure in his thoughts, in his words and in his deeds. He must remain unassailably himself. Henceforth he must assume full responsibility for his own development.

Paradoxically, the most elementary type of freedom on earth —merely to appear without disturbing anyone physically or verbally—is the freedom which is most easily challenged and eroded by the conventions imposed by human society in various places. The psychiatrist draws his first intimation of diagnosis of the psychopath from the clothes and other things which the patient puts on.

The African intoxicated and disoriented by his full exposure to Western civilization requires judicious reorientation from an informed, able and purposeful leadership. Strong-arm measures and curtailment of what is usually regarded as freedom of the individual will be indispensable in the endeavor to keep the African essentially African. An effective continental government or a continental opinion is best placed to carry out this invaluable mandate.

As more Africans become educated and see the rest of the world and know more about themselves, it will become increasingly unnecessary to advise them on certain very personal matters.

The question has to be asked once again, What must the African assert? What must he salvage of African culture, and why must he do away with certain aspects of his culture? How can he remain essentially himself without being oversentimental or ridiculous and without undermining the ideals of internationalism and universal common brotherhood and with good will to all nations and to all men? This is one of the crucial and perplexing question that often confront the African today, whether in government or as an individual in his professional or private life.

Internationalism and universal common brotherhood are great and good ideals so long as they would not in any way keep one nation or one brother permanently and inescapably under the other. But in the intense struggle of all brothers and nations, in all contexts and in all spheres, to survive and to attain the maximum security conceivable, the tendency for domination of one brother or nation by another is rendered inevitable. The nature of the domination may take any form: social, economic, political, religious or psychological. It is no wonder, therefore, that at times states and nations continue to exist only in name. They would stubbornly insist that they are cherishing their sovereignty even when obviously they are not doing so and cannot do so.

Were it not for this, it would have occurred to many desperately poor countries to apply to federate with or be completely unified with the richer nations of the world just because they want to increase their national income per capita. For the same reason some states in the Western Hemisphere would have yearned to join the United States; some of the former African and Asiatic colonies would have volunteered to return into the imperial fold, especially if this time there were adequate guarantees of equal and common citizenship, free movement of people and of capital and equal creative opportunities for all without any trace of racial or religious discrimination. There is no doubt at all that under such circumstances the income per capita of the poorer nations would soar astronomically in a matter of days, not years, and the material well-being, and social and welfare amenities, phenomenally improved.

But such a move usually is not made. There are certain instinctive and powerful factors. The first is pride, human, ancestral and national. The second is made up of instinctive fears. It appears to be a dangerous, unpredictable and an almost unworkable sell-out and smacks of defeatism and hopelessness. It would mean that the leaders have virtually sold their birthright for a mess of pottage—for materialism. Others, in their unalloyed and irrepressible loyalty to their ancestors and their fatherland, would insist that they can conserve their cultural heritage and still manage to improve the material well-being of their people. These conservatives are the real guardians of the national frontiers. Their instinct is to rebel, seriously and religiously, against any outside influences, especially when these would probably spell, sooner or later, domination in one form or another. It is this undefeated and undefeatable group that put a curb on internationalism. They are not necessarily against international cooperation and friendship. They are in abundance in every country everywhere. Among their chief proponents are often the heads of state and chief executives.

This is the obvious danger: that should an African country apparently sell out or surrender its sovereignty to a foreign country merely because it cannot materially continue to go it alone, should Africa as a continent practically sell out all its reserves and distinctions to Europe, America or Asia merely because it cannot materially cope alone, then the inescapable result would be continued and permanent African subjugation. Forever Africa would remain beyond redemption, and could never truly come into its own.

It is probably safe and meet for the nations of the New World to import the souls of Europe, Asia and Africa into their territories. This would matter little. The majority of these populations are immigrants from the Old World. Already the exercise has proved so successful that it is almost obsolete to belong to the Old World; all that appertains to the Old World appears archaic and dispensable. But in Africa, where the majority of the populations are the indigenous people, to actually jettison their soul and replace it with something completely extraneous would definitely result in a psychological defeat—a defeat brought about by excessive craving for materialism.

Therefore, to blithely dismiss the necessity for an African language or the invention of a national, regional, or continental script as being irrelevant, far too late, absolutely unnecessary or absurd is the very first step to admitting, once and for all time, that Africa is already beyond redemption, irretrievably swept into Europe, at least so far as languages and scripts are concerned.

To all right-thinking people it looks eminently difficult and impossible to achieve or retrieve African languages and scripts, for various reasons. Yet such achievements can be so vital and meaningful that they should always be examined carefully.

Some people once found it all too easy to condemn and censure attempts to vaccinate against smallpox with cowpox; some once lamented and scoffed at those who first suggested traveling by air; and some execrated those who first took unusual interest to see if America existed and those who first bothered unduly with whether the world was round, oblong or square. There was a time when people shook their heads at those who believed that human speech could be recorded and its shadow transmitted on television. There are those who, either through their ignorance or in their pathological defeatism, see nothing but an element of real madness in the scientist who spends all night in the laboratory; they keep wondering who sent him and what he is looking for and whether it is worth it. Experiments to go to the moon may be rated unnecessary and extravagant in view of other, pressing world or national problems to which such moneys are probably better diverted. The attempt to go to the moon may be motivated more by curiosity and thirst for knowledge than by any other consideration. But if the end result of a moon landing would actually be to improve the lot of man on earth (a thing hard to foretell), then it is worth it.

As these apply to science, so they apply to culture. If the end result of establishing an African language or script would be to improve the lot of the African of centuries hence, rather than to have them turned into speaking dummies and parrots who have nothing original and authentic to offer (a thing easy to foretell), then it cannot be absurd to canvas the continued existence of certain, or of all, African languages and also the invention or development of African scripts.

Things that do not begin sometime, somewhere, somehow, will never exist.

If it can be meet and right for Europeans, Asiatics, etcetera, to continue to be essentially themselves, living their own lives, wearing their own dress, speaking their own languages and indeed persisting in being essentially themselves, when they come into Africa or when they emigrate to other parts of the world, then there is a great deal to be said for the African's persisting in being himself essentially, not only while at home in Africa but also, and even more importantly, when he goes abroad.

Full African maturity and reclamation of lost ground in culture cannot be real and effective until the African, in the comity of nations, is able to rise and open his mouth to speak, to address the world, in a language which is distinctively African and of Africa's original choice. It is very doubtful whether the African can fully establish and exert his intrinsic personality and human resources to the maximum until he can appear and express himself in a way which is as natural and as authentic as possible.

In this age of unprecedented materialism, there is nothing in culture, yet there is everything in culture; there is nothing in language, yet there is everything in language; there is nothing in dress and appearance, yet there is everything in dress and appearance; there is nothing in name, yet there is everything in name; there is nothing in anything, yet there is everything in everything. Everything is lost. Anything and everything are borrowed. I am, in a way, a cipher, for there is nothing in me which is really me. I am no damned good to myself. I am a betrayal to my ancestors and a letdown to humanity and to posterity.

CHAPTER SIX

Tribalism and Democracy

All over Africa it soon became the fashion to prepare for independence. Constitutions, parliaments, ministries and cabinets, chancelleries and various ambitious national institutions were founded. Admission into the United Nations and other world bodies was enthusiastically granted for the asking. Flags, anthems and all the other paraphernalia found in any modern state were assembled. Then the spirit, the pride and the hope of these new African nations were built around these new things.

Well might we ask, In the years that political independence has become the rule rather than the exception throughout Africa, how have these countries measured up to the challenge? Has the independence of these states brought the sort of internal peace, progress, prosperity and hopefulness, the increased human dignity and international prestige, everyone had joyfully hoped for?

By the time the imperial powers left Africa, they had helped the indigenes of their various colonies to frame constitutions. Some constitutions never worked at all; some, after an initial trial, soon proved inexpedient and had to be drastically altered, often to a more totalitarian type.

Within five years politicians—colleagues and opponents alike —who had become prominent citizens by the twilight of the colonial era had been arrested, imprisoned or exiled in at least ten African countries. By 1966 civilian governments had succumbed, voluntarily or involuntarily, temporarily or indefinitely, to military regimes in six instances, four of these in quick succession within one month. Some opposition parties voluntarily folded up and cast their lot with the ruling party, with some of their members accepting cabinet posts. Nevertheless, the unassailable fact has emerged that all these various governments have been able to achieve far more for their respective countries in every field of economic and social development in five to ten years than the colonial powers did throughout the whole of their almost hundred years of rule in Africa.

Although disease, illiteracy and malnutrition are still rampant, with social amenities either grossly inadequate or sadly lacking and the level of human existence still terribly miserable, yet more schools, hospitals, roads, factories, opportunities and social amenities have appeared in areas where they had been undreamt of a decade before independence. Each of the countries, confidently or not, launched its own development program, often with the assistance of the old colonial master. Moreover, these new countries, through their political independence, have been able to exert some form of international influence, helping in the cause of world peace and universal human liberty.

Ideally, in these new African sovereign states national unity would imply not merely that the various families, villages, towns, ethnic or tribal groups within a geographical region had decided to sail or sink together in the same boat but also that everyone would possess the same measure of opportunity, share the same sense of belonging and be accorded an equal degree of freedom, individual liberty and creative opportunity in any square inch of that particular country. To the ordinary man in the street, as with the animal in the forest or the bird that roams the skies, it should not primarily matter from where the central direction came. Whether it emanated from a world government or a continental government, or from only one person, whether it was delegated through a regional, district or family administration, would be of only secondary significance. What would be supremely important remained the same: that after independence everyone lived a better, more prosperous and hopeful life, enjoyed a great degree of freedom of speech, and felt secure and free of domination in any form or guise.

At the Berlin and Brussels dissection of Africa that took place toward the close of the nineteenth century, the imperial powers, in delineating their spheres of influence, had, as much as they could, galvanized various ethnic groups on the continent to suit their own economic and administrative ends. The arbitrary boundaries drawn often severed peoples of the same linguistic, racial or religious group to serve under different imperial flags. Some of these groups today number in the thousands, others in the millions. The only bond between them, at least in recent history, resulted from their contiguity and European colonialism. Some of these groups had always been African nations in the same sense as there were nations in Europe and Asia. These African groups remain as distinct, one from another, as the French, the Russians, the Greeks, the Spaniards, the Dutch, are distinct and different among themselves. Indeed, these African groups are often peoples with unequal levels of social advancement and literacy, peoples with unequal economic resources and potentialities, peoples with different oral traditions, peoples with different economic, political, social, cultural, and religious institutions. *Tribe* is the contemptuous and cynical expression preferred by certain peoples, including some Africans, to refer to these African nations. Tribalism is the inherent ancestral and group sentiment manifested especially within the framework of these new European-made supranational bodies. Tribalism is nationalism.

During the colonial era, subjected to a common unpopular and unwanted regime, the inherent sectional loyalties within these various groups were either irrelevant or frivolous in the unanimous and resolute demand for self-government. As the various groups approached the constitutional conference tables, however, submerged sectionalism began to surface and get increasingly ominous. As colonialism was taking its exit through the front door, tribal chauvinism was flying in through the windows.

That tribalism should constitute such a potent force in Africa after the departure of colonialism should not be very surprising. In the New World, especially in North America, and in Australia, immigrants from Europe in recent centuries still cling, albeit subtly and instinctively, to their various ancestral European nations. The English, French, Irish, Italians and Poles, can still echo effectively in North American public life. Within these new African supranational entities, tribalism is fundamentally a defensive or protective instinct rather than a calculated attempt by the constituent nations to dominate their neighbors socially, culturally, politically, economically or otherwise. It often manifests group solidarity and insecurity rather than portray any other extraordinary vice or virtue. In short, it is a socio-psychological complex.

Since the attainment of independence in these territories, tribalism, along with nepotism and corruption, has proved one of the most intractable causes of internal strife and political instability; it has emerged as the exact antithesis of national unity. As a ready recourse, it has become the invigorating drink of the forsaken careerist and the callous trump card of the destitute politician. Equally it has matured as a terrible centrifugal and disruptive force, to fan the flames of secession, threatening the handicapped and intoxicating the privileged.

We can hardly help being what we already are as regards our various tribes or nations, any more than we can help belonging to a particular sex. We can hardly be ashamed of our ancestral heritage, which we might like to perpetuate in certain respects. But in so far as tribalism would callously rob Peter to pay Paul to maintain Paul's confidence, in so far as it would dismiss meritocracy in favor of mediocrity hoisted upon a tribal pole, in so far as it can be made to appear a substitute for talent, it must be regarded as an unmistakable instrument of injustice, oppression and frustration. Again, as long as tribalism remains a rather narrow-minded, overplayed and unrealistic feeling that hinders the socio-economic advancement of a people in a world in which fusion, the obliteration of national frontiers and the formation of large blocs is the preferred and even the only redeeming thing, tribalism must be regarded as a primitive, unfortunate and retrogressive influence.

But it would be rash to brush aside or underscore the patent inequalities and complexes among the constituent tribes of these new supranational bodies. The inequalities of population, education and resourcefulness engender, almost inevitably, genuine fears and apprehensions. The minority and handicapped groups are acutely sensitive to domination by the more populous, the more socially advanced or the more resourceful groups. They are afraid of replacing European imperialism with imperialism imposed by their neighbors. Thus, these not-so-fortunate groups would at least want their own fair share of national development: roads, schools, hospitals, scholarships, public appointments and so on. They would also like to see their sons share in government as it guides the destiny of their nations within the context of the supranational body, protecting their legitimate interests. They fear suppression and eventual eclipse of the ancestral heritage which they tend to guard jealously. Very few of these tribes or nations are confident enough to launch themselves independently into the international scene. They are virtually compelled, thanks to colonialism, to cooperate with one another: this is about the only way they can survive honorably and hopefully as peoples in the modern world. Nevertheless, for the purpose of personal security, the tribe remains the reassuring entity; the nation itself is a new being, unknown and untried.

In the setup of these supranational bodies the minority groups stand at a definite and permanent disadvantage. The neutral observer wonders at the monumental imbecility of the dwarf that has decided, or has been persuaded, to share the same room with a giant whose foot alone weighs more than the dwarf's whole body. Yet each is a mature being, capable of an independent existence, however precarious.

In effect, wherever tribalism is a potent force and certain groups regard themselves as numerically, economically or socially inferior to others, the definition and the concept of democracy, or democratic government, becomes extremely controversial. If we are to accept democracy—the age-old concept which has been given various definitions and manipulated by various peoples at various periods for various purposes—to mean simply government of the people by the people for the people, in modern

Africa certain questions must be asked immediately as to who these people are. Are they individual citizens who, one by one, share a common identity and possess equal loyalty to the country, or are they in fact individuals already deeply committed to their tribal units who would cast their votes en bloc in favor of a kinsman in a country-wide election in spite of the kinsman's obvious incompetence and poor record? The better-qualified and more competent fellow just happens to have come from the wrong tribe. Unless the various tribes enjoy equal representation in parliament irrespective of their population, size and economic resourcefulness, then the victory of the larger tribes over the smaller ones in any country-wide election is a foregone conclusion. Even before going to the polls, the larger tribes can assume that with their built-in majority, the chief executive and the majority of the cabinet would come from them.

In practice, therefore, these quantitatively or qualitatively handicapped tribes are little better than permanently subject nations, and their destiny is virtually in the hands of peoples who are somewhat foreign to them and who are rather different from them in certain important respects. It is incredible that even after decades of sharing the same European tutelage and after centuries of coexistence in the same region of Africa, these nations are often ignorant of one another's way of life, with very little interpenetration and social intercourse. One of the principal tragedies of colonialism was the development of a system of communication which served to move the various peoples and their ways of life closer to Europe: instead of interlocking the diverse peoples, colonial roads and railways invariably led to the sea and toward Europe.

The Seeds on Barren Land

In some older nations in Europe and North America where parliamentary democracy has become established, it was never attained in months or years but over several decades and centuries. With it grew such parallel forces as an independent judiciary, an influential and independent press, an informed and influential middle class, and organic literate masses who are politically conscious and knowledgeable about the outside world. At times such masses went through the physical and mental agonies of war in their own lifetime, and thus learned of the suffering and privations which their ancestors had endured in recent centuries. They are mature masses with inspired pressure groups which are greatly dedicated to causes which they believe to be true and right. Moreover, in a few of these countries the monarchy is a revered institution in itself, often nationally regarded as a neutral arbiter.

In the newly created nations of Africa these factors, some of which in themselves are prerequisites or essential ingredients of parliamentary democracy, are sadly missing—at least for some time yet. The press is quite often weak and biased, partly because it is usually an organ of a political party from which partisan warfare is reflected to the masses. There are very few presses in Africa which have an editorial staff of such neutrality, objectivity and brilliance as will influence the opinion of politicians or sway the masses one way or another.

The over-all effect is for politicians to assume their puritanic posture and brazen-facedly ignore and dismiss the press. They would undertake the swaying of the masses with their own oratorical promises, swearings and boasts, with threats and victimizations directed at the constituencies; indeed, they could simply resort to organized gangsterism. This obvious lack of respect on the part of politicians for the intelligence, knowledge and integrity of the ordinary people, and this open disregard for the potential influence and power of the masses, form a disturbing aspect of freedom and liberty in the developing countries. In most instances there are as yet no country-wide traditions, no precedents and no national ethics, as are in existence in the older democracies.

The political leaders and the masses are therefore unlikely to show the sort of political understanding and good will involved in smoothly surrendering power to an opponent after an election defeat, as is commonly done in Western Europe and in the New World, where parliamentary democracy has become traditional. The man called upon to surrender power has little or no guarantee that his opponent will be just as willing to abdicate when it comes to his turn. Hence, unless some referee is present to ensure fair play, especially at general elections, the tendency is for a political party to continue to enjoy power forever. Whereas in the far-advanced countries the informed masses constitute this referee and the final court of appeal for the warring political parties, in the developing countries, in a world in which non-interference in others' internal affairs is a maxim which at least enjoys universal lip service, events in the mid-60's showed that the local army is the only honest broker, the guardian of the constitution. Perhaps a very embittered people who would rise, almost spontaneously, and demonstrate against the injustices being done to them could also serve the same purpose. Indeed, until law and order have actually broken down and the government has lost its control over the masses, it can hardly be forced to surrender power even when it has obviously lost a nation-wide election.

The transfer of power in the new nations is thus an extraordinarily delicate matter and calls for the type of reciprocal partisan confidence that would have made an opposition party quite unnecessary in the first place. Where this confidence is lacking, it is only the law (if it can be enforced) or the impartiality of the armed forces (if they can be impartial) that has any hope of averting nation-wide political strife. To call on any outside power would automatically embroil the country in power politics.

Surely, what is at stake in Africa is not democracy. African governments must preoccupy themselves with any means conducive to peace, progress, prosperity, efficiency and practical fair play among the tribes and peoples in their lands.

The Palliative Measures

Tribalism in any African nation is a cancer that lurks ominously in the national body; it is bound to prove a serious handicap to the nation's health and even strike its death blow. The immediate tragedy of tribalism is that it makes nepotism, bribery and corruption on a country-wide basis inevitable; tribalism becomes a way of life.

The real challenge presented by the political independence granted to these rather vague unions of tribes or nations that form the new independent African states is for them to synthesize a fraternity that will create implicit country-wide confidence—to construct a supranational edifice which is reliable and durable, full of equal promise and equal creative opportunities for all and keeping all citizens in its warm embrace irrespective of tribe, tongue, creed or culture.

The fundamental aim in any progressive African country must be to find a way of coping with tribalism—containing it as it is or eradicating its obnoxious and offensive tendencies. Of course, a dictatorship, if it wishes—and if it is progressive it must wish—with its drastic and uncompromising measures, stands a far greater chance of actually extirpating tribalism and galvanizing the country into one solid unit than does any other form of government.

If, primarily, on the other hand, there must be a liberal democratic government, then sufficient allowance must be made for any obstacles that might visibly stand in the way of a healthy and workable association among the diverse peoples.

Should only a halfhearted attempt be made to weld incompatibles together, it would only foster perennial internal friction and instability and retard the pace of socio-economic development. It can be no copybook affair when it comes to designing a constitution for peoples in any region of the world: one river, one mountain, one mine, one creed, one historical incident, one foreign doctrine, one leader, one race, here or there could be the crucial factor in determining the failure or success of the so-called unitary, federal or confederal government or other form of administration.

If there must be representative government with members of every tribe sharing in decision making at the central powerhouse, then the unit to be represented must not lead to domination by any one tribe. There are four obvious lines to pursue.

First, the unitary form of government. Here the larger tribes must be divided into smaller units roughly equal in size, population or viability. This prescription will generate a degree of intratribal rivalry with no real tribal hero; tribal solidarity will automatically be undermined and will be compromised in the supranational interest; intertribal goodwill between the large and the small tribes will become a more likely proposition. Such units must be weak and essentially dependent upon the supranational body. These units are viable only in so far as they exist administratively—*not* ethnically, culturally, economically, religiously or otherwise. They exist only constitutionally, as part of the whole country or supranational body of which they form just another administrative denominator. They do not exist as any whole or as a state that would be able, economically or developmentally, to go it alone, paying its own way, maintaining its own ministers and all and enjoying residual powers. All residual powers must be vested in a strong central government. The stronger the central government, the better for national cohesion and purposefulness.

But as long as each tribe continues to possess an unalloyed spirit and solidarity or continues to be susceptible (almost religiously) to only one hero, the country—the supranational body— can never command the maximum loyalty possible. Again, as long as any of the bigger tribes can always be easily rallied under one flag, their solidarity remains a constant advantage over the smaller groups and their confidence in an easily viable secession remains a constant source of supranational instability. Indeed, unless the larger tribes, especially, are divided each one against itself, so that it will not stand as one unit, the country itself, the supranational body, remains an unstable entity.

Second, a federal type of government, with states based strictly on tribal or linguistic lines. The constituent tribes will enjoy considerable autonomy with residual powers, but the country—the supranational body—will share a common market, a common currency, a co-ordinated economic and industrial development plan. The tribes will participate as equals in the statutory bodies and in other institutions, such as higher education, which each unit cannot by itself well afford. This collection of states will probably need to formulate a common foreign-policy and defense plan and present itself to the rest of the world as a single entity with only one voice and (at least apparently) one destiny. It will be essential to have a council of ministers with equal representation from each of the constituent states to elect the president or secretary general, who will hold office not indefinitely but for terms of two to four years, in rotation amongst the states. The council of ministers will also look after the institutions of common interest. There will be free movement of trade and of manpower, but peoples from different states will not expect equal treatment as regards creative opportunities outside their respective states. Under this type of federal government the pivot of democratic election will lie in the constituent state, where candidates may stand election as independents or as party nominees.

Third, a confederation with even looser ties among the states, with perhaps only a common market and communication.

Fourth, each tribe or nation will be completely independent and develop autonomously, without much regard to its neighbors.

Needless to say, the last three systems promote tribal solidarity and make for unnecessary duplication and competitiveness. They beg the questions posed by tribalism rather than attempting to solve them. While they may create intertribal peace and good-neighborliness, they are far from being the most efficient system to promote the socio-economic growth of that region of Africa or even of the various tribes concerned.

Party Politics and Tribalism

All too often certain experts claim that political parties are indispensable in a mass democracy. This viewpoint cannot apply to Africa. In its young countries, made up of distinct tribal groups, party politics will, first and foremost, tend to accentuate tribalism and other centrifugal factors.

It must be recalled that all over Africa, on the eve of independence, political parties were born primarily to harass colonialism and strive for self-government. These were the truly militant organizations which by and large received the blessing of practically all citizens. The immediate issue then was simple, magnetic and magical: self-government. Then, the threat of foreign rule was either very obvious or easily revealed. The desire to fight it among the various peoples to whom it constituted a common danger was so intense that differences were submerged and the peoples were easily rallied together. Any disagreement that led to the formation of splinter groups could nearly always be traced to someone's personal ambition or to petty quarrels among certain leaders who, either for their own advantage or on account of the threat to the security and buoyancy of their tribal groups after colonialism, would fight for tribal or regional autonomy or even for secession away from the rest. Indeed, the opportunist only had to wave his magic wand of tribalism, and his tribal, rather than party, manifesto would appear; the tune was all too reminiscent of the Pied Piper of Hamlin. The type of proliferation was endless and spelled a potential setback to stable government both on the national and on the regional level in any African country where it occurred. As colonialism was liquidated the major national parties tended to shrink into tribal parties, each one constrained and contenting itself with maintaining only its toe holds on the others' territories, territories with jealously guarded emotional and cultural frontiers.

It must be noted that religious differences have not, so far, proved a potent political force in any of the new African countries. Muslims, Christians, pagans, animists, agnostics, atheists, all willingly share the same cabinet table. But should religious differences become significant, for example to the extent of affecting political parties, then that country would have another serious problem to cope with, the dimensions of which may even be greater than those of tribalism.

Again, workers' parties are liable to be easily swept away by the force of tribalism, but should they arise, in spite of the established parties already claiming that they represent all segments of the population, then these workers' parties are still liable to fall victim to the same built-in centrifugal force of tribalism, sooner or later, assuming that they have the financial resources to last long enough, in view of the crippling poverty in these countries.

Of course, in essence, party politics presumes that some time, maybe in years or decades, the opposition party can come to wield power or come to share in it in that country. Without this hope followership will thin out and the party eventually disappear.

In most African countries it is quite striking that the major country-wide parties invariably stand for the same ideals, if they care to proclaim any. Since the departure of colonialism there has been no really new magnetic force to rally the various peoples together, apart from the unanimous demand for unity and speedy development. The new parties often have nothing irrestibly attractive or new to offer. In some of the countries, political parties preach national unity and condemn secession while in the same breath watering the tree of tribalism to insure their survival.

These different political parties came about, not so much because they had something really different to offer but because it was the fashionable thing, especially in the imperial countries that gave birth to them.

The misconception grew that politics meant parties.

It is very doubtful whether political parties existed in indigenous African political institutions. Everyone usually belonged, as a matter of course, to the same body politic.

Party politics was imported into Africa by Africans trained in Europe and America, and the colonial governments were often ready to encourage these cleavages and mutually antagonistic entities.

Undoubtedly all political parties would want to see their people better fed, better housed and better clothed; they would strive to outbid one another in their offers of freedom of speech, thought and association.

In developing countries, especially in Africa, there are several cogent factors which make the multiple-party system or government, with a sworn opposition party, less advantageous, less reasonable and less logical than a single-party or a submerged-party or a no-party system.

First, there are as yet few educated citizens capable of running the country efficiently. It obviously is wise to make the best use of all the brain-power resources the country can possibly muster. This is most important. Local intellectuals must be able to hold their own with or against their foreign counterparts at any international combat. The country can ill afford to ignore some of the very few knowledgeable people simple because they sympathized with the wrong political parties.

Second, it often is found that even in the far-advanced countries, for example in Europe and North America, coalition governments are formed in times of such national emergencies as wars, earthquakes and floods; old political enmities are suspended and every citizen rallies to support the current ruler even though they may not fully endorse the cause for which he is fighting in the name of the nation. Ordinarily it is almost a rule in the far-advanced countries where there is parliamentary democracy to present a somewhat united front in foreign policy. In any country an excellent image of internal peace and stability serves to promote favorable economic relations with the outside world.

Third, all African countries must logically regard themselves as already mobilized into a state of emergency, an emergency that will last a matter of decades. These countries are so terribly far behind that should they adopt any other attitude, they will never succeed in raising the living standard of their peoples to a decent level in the foreseeable future. All possible hands must therefore be united on deck. Hence, the best prescription for stable, resolute, efficient and progressive government in a developing country is a system that will tend to generate unanimity and national purposefulness rather than animosities and sectional interests among peoples who have sworn to one another to share a common destiny.

Fourth, the whole of Africa is in a state of emergency now, and will be for at least the rest of this century, and the continent can ill afford to debate trivialities or tolerate the inordinate and selfish ambitions of career politicians, who often are more interested in fighting for their own personal security than in anything else. The issue at stake in modern Africa is painfully obvious to all and sundry—"peace, progress, prosperity and a better life for all." Certainly it is not the means to attain this objective that elude anyone or cause disagreements sharp enough to call for the formation of political parties.

Fifth, not only does the official opposition party tend to seize upon and feel almost obliged to oppose or criticize all issues, even the best ones, but it has already set itself up as a target to the government as a bunch of unmistakable political enemies who are out to taunt, ridicule or even hinder the socio-economic endeavors of the government. The vindictive spirit of the opposition when it attains power is the greatest nightmare of all to the government of the day: the opposition is likely to have its own back on the retiring government and its supporters, with such witch hunting as may involve every aspect of national life.

Sixth, the opposition parties, unless aided from outside, can be kept going only at very personal sacrifice coupled with the courage and reliance of their convictions. There are no moneys bequeathed to political parties nor any other sources of income to ensure their smooth running. The masses, and especially the influential middle class, are still so economically insecure in themselves that they will invariably flow in the same direction as the current of prosperity. Very often the opposition parties are unable to make their views known to the country. They can neither establish branches, run a newspaper nor appeal to the electorate as adequately as can the government party. In many instances they run up against commercial competition with the government party. On the whole it is far better not to expend men and money in running a political party at all if that party cannot be effectively run so as to appear a likely alternative to the government of the day.

Seventh, there is widespread social insecurity in developing African countries. The cash, and the levers to control wealth and property, are almost all at the command of the government of the day. These factors in themselves go to make the formation of political parties opposed to the government party quite a frustrating and hazardous exercise.

Eighth, the opposition party may grow so hopeless of gaining power that it becomes ineffective and may be tempted to seek foreign financial and even military support. Soon suspicions, plots and fabrications begin to pollute the air. Of all the continents there is none so susceptible to the political and financial influences of other continents as Africa most unfortunately is. This is one of the greatest calamities of party politics in Africa. The diversity of ethnic groups in each of the countries coupled with the prevalent poverty and the individual and collective social insecurity provides opportunities to external mischief makers to an extent unknown anywhere else in the world.

Patriotism is a feeling, not a profession. Politicians are not necessarily the most loyal patriots, but they often are the most ostentatious and vociferous advocates of their own viewpoints.

That there is an appreciable degree of self-interest and personal aggrandizement in every politician cannot be gainsaid; this is perhaps understandable and natural, however genuinely one would like to live a life of service. When, however, politics has to be the only means of livelihood, when in fact the politician has no other profession or job to fall back upon, to deprive him of his only source of income, especially when this has been substantial or promising, must be a dreadful blow indeed that will be averted at almost any cost. This situation attains an unprecedented pitch among the career politicians in some of the new nations of Africa. Most of them were either unemployed or underemployed. The desire and fight for political power is not actually a function of patriotism or of dedication to a particular development program, it is not, as one might normally like to believe, motivated by a desire for an honorable place in history, nor is it inspired by a sense of mission. It is more a desperate struggle to live, and to ensure personal security and family security and if possible tribal security. Tribal affiliation is used to buy personal security, and this is then used in return to buttress the tribe and keep it alive as a reservoir of votes to ensure personal security. Once political power is attained, it has to be consolidated. This may involve increasing that power on the one hand, while on the other systematically disarming and impoverishing and even buying over the opposition parties. Corruption and repression in all forms and guises are therefore inevitable.

The Constructive and Vigilant Opinion

It is therefore the tolerance, dedication and selflessness of politicians that must be of greatest moment if they are really to have the over-all interest of the nation at heart, rather than their abiding faith in this or that political doctrine or pattern of development.

Disagreement will always exist among political leaders, just as they do among educationists, industrialists, churchmen, soldiers, club members, families and any other groupings of people. That disagreements arise should not automatically mean that political parties must be hatched ot advocate the various divergent points of view; if this were so, then theoretically there would be as many political parties as there are individuals. But realists as politicians often are, in their attempt to appear to the world as parts of a probable alternative to the government of the day, they are inexorably drawn into only one or two blocs, never into too many ineffective blocs.

Opposition parties are sanctuaries for conscientious dissenters and objectors; they are watchdogs of the people which, in their zealousness to be in power in the foreseeable future, form bodies that would study the details of government proposals and if possible challenge, criticize and suggest amendments or alternatives to them. They are defenders of the people against any excesses of the government of the day, keeping that government on its toes, never complacent, never careless, never reckless. In spite of these strong points in favor of their existence, opposition parties must be regarded as an obvious luxury—a waste of the too few educated people and a waste of valuable time—in the less developed countries of the world. The case is not that the principle of having opposition parties is bad or useless but that in desperate countries with perplexing problems they do more harm than good. Such countries are better off without them.

While the existence of opposition parties is an indication of government tolerance and of freedom of expression and association, this freedom can be real and meaningful only at a certain stage of socio-economic advancement of the people. Is it of any use to brandish freedom of speech, of expression, of association, of worship, to a mass of hopelessly poor, hungry, homeless and ignorant illiterates? Little would they imagine that they are in fact a deprived, incoherent, unconscious and moribund lot. Even when he is free to speak his mind, what sort of contribution or criticism can the ignorant illiterate make in the modern world, of which he understands so very little or of which he is totally unconscious? What sort of liberty can the African laborer who owes his very livelihood and daily bread and survival and those of his family to his master really have? While these wonderful ideals must always be borne at heart, the first essential step is to raise the general socio-economic standard of the people and disseminate *fundamental human knowledge* before laying emphasis on enunciating *fundamental human rights* which are useless and hypocritical in the context. In European and North American countries, with their far-advanced socio-economic standards, freedom of speech, association and worship have evolved over the centuries and are now so customary that they are almost irrepressible.

In the modern closely knit world the alertness and opinion of the rest of mankind is, all by itself, a massive opposition party—watching, spying, prying, supporting, bullying, reporting, trying, cautioning, restraining, challenging, and in places condoning, the government in power. Every responsible government is quite aware of this, that it is a cynosure of the rest of the world, be it a weak or a strong country.

Party politics would not always guarantee that even party members could express themselves freely within the party caucus or challenge the party leadership, even when their conscience compels them to do so. Partisanship is the first evidence of failure of the national leaders to unite for the common good of their people, more so when there is a state of emergency, as in contemporary Africa.

The real gem of freedom of speech and liberty in any country is the freedom to express one's own belief and not be persecuted as a result of exercising this fundamental human right. African countries, rather than religiously aiming to please the rest of the world or to pretend that they can exactly copy parliamentary democracy or this or that form of democracy as found in the East or in the West, must simply content themselves with ensuring that they have the requisite capacity to accommodate criticisms from their own populations.

To suppress an opposition political party may not be a wrong thing, but to suppress informed opinion—the intellectuals, the professionals, the press—in any form, by direct or indirect threats, especially when these have been independent, discreet and sufficiently diplomatic in the national interest, is an overtly oppressive and unwise rule. It is a shattering blow to freedom and a flagrant denial of fundamental human rights. The aim of the opposition party is significantly different from that of these other groups. The opposition political party is determined that it shall one day come into power. It is already a shadow government, with real and proclaimed political ambitions and as such a potential source of subversion and a pawn to any extraneous influences that may be ready to throw their vicious hooks and baits into muddy waters.

Because of the illimitable influence, power and aspirations of the greater powers, because of the poverty, relative ignorance and poorer knowledge of general affairs prevalent in the backward countries, any obvious disunities and cleavages in these poor little dears are easily exploited to suit the whims and caprices of the greater powers.

The one-party system of government implies that all must, by legislation, belong together in one political fold and that any dissident individuals or groups are to be punished for breaking the law of the land. Ideally this presumes that the only party of the nation must be such as will tolerate and contain all forms of divergent views within it and not expel or admonish anyone or any fraction that disagrees with the rest on issues that may crop up from time to time. Hundreds of issues are to be discussed, and it is humanly impossible to expect unanimity on every issue raised.

Within the single party, factions will emerge and collect themselves around personalities, ideologies, tribes or nationalities, foreign influences, personal susceptibilities and vanities. It is impossible to imagine that all factions will differ on all the issues at stake. Apart from a declaration of war or the surrender of sovereignty, one can hardly imagine any issue controversial enough to make a faction walk out implacably—surely not issues of unity, progress, prosperity and the better life, which all must be the overwhelming preoccupation in every developing country. All patriots, if they are true and modest, must be capable of co-operating within the framework of a one-party system.

The various ways to discipline factions in a one-party system are unlikely to differ appreciably from those required in any of the better-organized parties under a plural-party system.

In a single-party state the opposing factions are permanently available to one another within the body politic, and they are less liable to become irreconcilable enemies. Various views are put forward for discussion, and success in pushing issues through will be an index of the political adroitness of any individual or faction. Freedom of discussion is manifested from inside the party. All the arguments that need to be are thrashed out within the party. The minority groups on particular national issues can win their way if they show adroitness.

Indeed, one of the fundamental arguments against partisan politics is that it is liable to create, encourage and multiply enmities among the people. Ordinary people are prejudiced even before they confront one another. In parliament they detest and loathe one another from the habitual and reflex disagreements to which they have committed and sworn themselves. They are allergic to one another's best suggestions and are heavily immunized to one another's true and better sides. They dwell (or duel) in mutual suspicion, not in mutual trust.

It is not an easy task at all to define what constitutes a dictator. One does not need to have seized the army and the judiciary before becoming one. It would of course be ridicuolus to make every appointment by voting or even by merely picking lots. But the very fact that a chief executive, once he has been voted into power in a free and fair election, can exercise his own discretion, all alone, to appoint his cabinet from his own party or from the whole country, and then exercise his own discretion to distribute other cabinet posts and make scores of other key appointments connotes a form of dictatorship in all but name. Having gained ascendancy to power, the chief executive can remain there until he is able to arrange for another general election. Through clever maneuvers he can tranquilize his opponents (both within and outside his own party) by rendering them politically impotent citizens or by persuading them into a form of dignified political exile such as an ambassadorship in some distant country. In the poorer countries the opposition is likely to swallow such sugar-coated pills; in the far-advanced and richer countries, however, there are enough opportunities available, and the prime minister's or president's offer can safely be turned down.

It is invariably an unfair practice to pass judgment on a government with only one word. Qualifications are always needed, for the lines can be extremely difficult to draw. When is a government benevolent or weak, radical or responsible, moderate or inefficient, tyrannical or strict, left, right of center, honest or foolish, clever, fraudulent or diplomatic? When is it lucky or unlucky (with the circumstances not of its own doing)? When has it failed on its own or been let down or subverted from outside? When is the government good or bad for the people, and what are the criteria for the assessments and by whom are they applied and in whose best interests?

All too often one wonders exactly what system any statesman from Europe, North America or Asia would unreservedly adopt if he were asked to govern any of the emergent African countries in the very best interests of that country and its generations yet unborn. How would he tackle such burning issues as tribalism, poverty, economic and social development, economic and cultural independence, capital formation, nationalization of foreign monopolies, trade with the richer countries, communism, capitalism, African unity, human rights, freedom?

Furthermore, one often wonders how many marks each former imperial country, or any other nation, would, in transparent honesty, award to the various governments in Africa on the ways they have guided the destiny of their respective countries, especially in the first five years of political independence, with mainly civilian governments at the helm, before the wave of army coups that swept away some of those governments.

The risks of a dictatorship are as well known as they are easily imagined. If dictatorships can guarantee and maintain their own honesty, benevolence and efficiency, then they are one of the best forms of government. This unfortunately is seldom the case. Given any country, it is almost purely a matter of luck whether a dictatorship will or can lapse into a tyranny or not.

The dictator who lets 1 per cent of his population suffer but is able to improve the lot of the rest by bringing peace, progress and national prosperity and stability into a country of twenty million, while he and his colleagues neither amass wealth nor allow others to do so—is he a better chief executive, in the long run, than the leader who, to maintain himself in power, condones (or is ineffective against) bribery and corruption at all levels, while, even though there is no curb on freedom of speech and association, 99 per cent of the population suffer not physical imprisonment but social and moral imprisonment, with misery, unemployment, ill health, hunger and pain, a high infant-mortality rate and hopeless poverty? Certainly the best leader of all is he who is able to bring progress and prosperity without having to crush his political opponents.

Military government established either as a result of a *coup d'état* or of civilian government voluntarily surrendering political power to the army, is a form of one-party hierachy. Soldiers as a group ascend to power, just as it would be possible for any other groups of professionals—churchmen, doctors, hunters, athletes, navy, students, scientists, bomb manufacturers—to crystallize from the general population as a distinctive set, with a common commitment or a common discipline. The army is potentially, but only visibly, and only perhaps, the strongest of such groups of professionals. Because it can, more easily than any other group, maintain the peace by actually frightening every other section of the population with the type of force and knowledge already at its disposal, it has the most obvious potentiality to lord it over all others. Whether it is in fact capable of governing the masses, bringing them peace, happiness, security and prosperity, with or without the cooperation of other professionals, is another proposition altogether. But the army remains an exclusive club or party, not allowing membership to all and sundry in all walks of life.

Workers too have their own power. Their party can be quite exclusive; their strikes can cripple the nation and force the rest of the population to its knees. And what of churchmen, scientists, doctors, etcetera?

The masses—all the people—of all walks of life, have the final power in the maintenance of peace and in the cooperation that makes life possible and progressive. They are led by politicians who are professional schemers and deliberators—or call them accredited intellectuals and a reasonably well informed group. The politicians accept all the risks and responsibilities involved in leadership and in guiding the destiny of the nation. The armed forces, the scientists, the workers, etcetera, are those who accept or content themselves with their role of helping the politicians in their task which, when properly performed, must be onerous.

All in all, in any type of government, whatever the political ideology and whatever the stage of socio-economic development of the people, the most crucial factor is he who is at the pinnacle of power at any given time. How this person got there, how he maintains his balance there, for how long he intends to stay there—all these other questions are of only secondary significance.

If he is generally unpopular, then the whole country either is condemned to serve its term under him or must find a way to get rid of him by persuasion or by force.

If this leader can be absolutely sure that his people do not want him any longer, as they show by their votes (if these can be valid) or by demonstrations and other means of protesting (if these are normally allowed), he will be more inclined to resign, especially if he is sure he has no dirty linen to hide or vendettas in store for him.

In the Western democracies the checks and balances of parliamentary democracy and such other built-in factors as the press, informed opinion and in particular the fact that the head of the national government is almost always sure that opposition against him has not been engineered from outside and indeed that his own people are rising against him out of their own genuine and logical feelings (for example, as indicated by an opinion poll)— all these make it easy and honorable for him to know when exactly to bow out.

In Africa and some other developing countries, however, this situation of an easy and voluntary abdication of power is less likely to be found. The fact is this, that the whole game of politics and the major aspects of national development in developing countries take place under the scorching surveillance of the great powers, who often find it difficult, because of the nature of power politics itself, to abstain from the goings on. The first definite result is internal mistrust and nervousness. Even when a leader has been ousted, by whatever means, he or his followers will invariably put the blame on such foreign influences as "imperialists" or "Communists."

Conclusion

In the exercising of political power the only thing that can be universally condemned is to take human life, for it lacks in degree. The other ideas which the world harps upon and yearns for and which are usually regarded as sine qua nons of a liberal kindly government vary in degree and are never absolute. They must be given their due consideration only after peace, stability and national security have been fully protected.

Freedom, within the context of speech, expression, conscience, movement and association, in any country is often regarded as one of the greatest demands and perhaps one of the inalienable rights of the people. Yet freedom is one of the most easily abused things that can be placed at the disposal of man. Freedom must be measured to meet the circumstances and needs of the environment in question and thus cannot have a universal value in any context.

African countries, themselves as countries, are not free as certain European and North American countries are free. They are not free enough to pursue certain courses without looking nervously left and right, whereas the more powerful countries may only look down to see how the weaker countries react to their policies, internal and foreign, and how they react to issues of mutual interest.

Within each country there must be freedom *in excelsis*, but freedom must never run counter to national, social and moral security, and it must never run counter to discipline, orderliness, planning, unity and conformity, for each of these is by itself often as great a standard as freedom, in the over-all well-being of the nation.

The amount of "freedom" that prevails within any country is a function of governmental carelessness, inefficiency or overconfidence at the one extreme of the spectrum, to governmental nervousness and insecurity at the other hand.

Within a party, freedom to vote, for example in parliament,

ranges from the restraint and loyalty that amounts to stupid, irresponsible and disgraceful acquiescence to the other extreme at which the members become indisciplined or uncooperative, with perennial threats of resignations and splits.

The head of a family knows how much freedom he can allow each member, including himself; likewise, heresy, vulgarity, pornography, unparliamentary language and so on are evidences for the restrictions which society must impose for the sake of decency or conformity.

In the developing countries of Africa a good deal depends on the discretion and judgment of the government and its head. They are to measure for themselves where freedom of the press, of speech and of association must start, and they must be able to pinpoint where these begin to constitute palpable danger to the community.

CHAPTER SEVEN

The Government and the People in Developing Countries

In Africa and other developing countries what is important is not whether there is a dictator as such but whether the chief executive is benevolent or malevolent, whether there is corruption, whether there is free access to courts of law, and whether these courts are free and fair. Another significant point is who, in any case, is passing judgment and in whose interest. African countries must be competent and able to alienate themselves from the opinion of others; they must be self-opinionated. The crucial factor therefore lies in an informed opinion which can be freely expressed.

The head of government has two major tasks: the one, to govern; the other, to ensure, beyond any shadow of doubt, a smooth and peaceful succession or alternative to himself. The second task is at least as important as the first, and demands due calculation.

The head of government must be a great pragmatist, a realist, who is also able to make wise use of other people's wisdom. Whether he would become authoritarian depends upon various factors. First, his own dexterity. Whatever the constitution, his own personal attitude to it and his own personal perspective on various aspects of goverment are of great moment. Second, his place among his lieutenants—how much influence he can exert on them severally and collectively, and how much in return these can stand up to influence him. The caliber, moral courage, foresight, alertness and honesty of his colleagues also come into full play. Has each one the courage of his convictions? Are these aides career politicians, dependent on their jobs as their sole means of livelihood? Other important factors include the alertness, courage, candor, brilliance and independence of the press and the pre-existing climate of free press and free speech. Nor can the masses be ignored. How much in fact is the government in any way afraid of the masses? Are they politically conscious—conscious to the extent of recognizing and reacting appropriately to lies, truths, half-truths, bribery and corruption? Will they defy a curfew and go to jail? Will they readily demonstrate against an unpopular measure?

In the mind's eyes, accurate and imaginative as it can be, it is the personality of the man at the pinnacle of power that is projected abroad. In an inexplicable way he soon emerges as the sole embodiment of his nation, its peoples, its wealths, its capabilities, its hopes and aspiration, its esthetics, etcetera. His own destiny is almost synonymous with the destiny of the whole nation, and his tenure of office can set the clock of social and economic advancement backward or forward by decades.

Consciousness of the imperishable influence of history books is a potent moralizing force in any nation. The more the leaders in public life are acutely aware of this incredibly powerful force, the more responsible and dedicated they are liable to become. For a leader to deal with the present as if the present will be judged only by those present here and today is the first evidence of incompetence, shallowness and shortsightedness. Such a leader is likely to stand in a remote place in history compared with the calculating pragmatist who rules with eyes set simultaneously on this moment and also on decades or even centuries hence, the leader who acts with a clairvoyant historical sense. As this pragmatic leader is contending with history, he, being human, is unable to disregard contemporary world opinion. He is eager to make his impact felt in distant lands, to be universally acclaimed, genuinely admired, respected and even feared.

The ideal public figure is a man of honor and esteem. His religious beliefs may in fact not be as great a solace and fortitude to him as the high premium he places on the immortality of history and the legacy of name which he is likely to bequeath to his descendants and to the world at large. He knows full well that every day, and even every moment, history is being made and that he himself is always playing a prominent part in this history.

He is painfully aware that his performance today could echo for centuries to come and his present role might be subjected to microscopic scrutiny and analysis at various centers the world over. He knows that his own grandchildren and everyone, anywhere, can eventually get to know the real truth of any matter. He knows his career could become the subject of an exhaustive and impartial thesis. If he succumbs to temptation, he will go any lengths to clear his name or make well-measured amends.

He is therefore meticulous in the role he plays and the standards he upholds. He makes sure that unalloyed honesty, love, devotion and charity pervade all deliberations. He would not like his own grandchildren to open the records and shed tears or be ashamed of him in his role, whether as a professor, statesman, minister of religion, explorer, scientist, benefactor or trade unionist. He perceives himself in different contexts— humanity, the nation, the race, the tribe, the family, the town, himself. All must be satisfied somehow—but how? His earthly wealth, his bank books, are to him of only little significance— quite ephemeral compared with the history books into which he is pouring all his investments. And when greatly inspired and overjoyed by the mystifying bliss in store for him he would claim to himself that he is filled with a sense of mission.

Such dedicated and responsible citizens are desperately needed in Africa and indeed throughout the world. At best this generation in Africa can do no better than attempt to set a solid foundation for the future and consolidate its political independence. It is only in this way that future generations can be truly proud of themselves and of their ancestors.

CHAPTER EIGHT

African Independence

Even though the transfer of power from the imperial country to the new African government was always a peaceful,
friendly and often sentimental affair loaded with promises on
both sides to maintain friendly relations, after independence the
first African dream was shattered upon realization of the im-
practicability of severing relations with the imperial country if
ever the African country contemplated doing so.

The imperial penetration into the African fabric had been far
deeper than anyone realized. The new countries were enmeshed
in a net of such Gordian ramifications that it was absolutely
futile, if not suicidal, to attempt to make an abrupt escape. The
imperial countries had actually given birth to children of their
own blood and their own image and even character. Whether
these children were legitimate or not remained immaterial—they
were born, once and for all. These children continued to exist
whether one liked them or hated them. They were in existence
even if they themselves regretted the circumstances of their own
birth. They had to survive, grow and seek their own independent
existence somehow, or perish.

These new countries had been immersed neck-deep in the
waters of colonialism. Independence in effect meant that only
the head and the feet could be allowed out of the pool while
the trunk was still firmly entrenched. The Guinea republic
courageously tried and nearly drowned, but was lucky to have a
timely rescue. After independence in many a country, the former
imperial powers endeavored to maintain the status quo and perpetuate their economic, military, cultural and technical influence.

They continue to break fresh frontiers (a process which some have cynically referred to as "give and keep"). They would view with resentment any active competition from the newer powers, notably the United States, Japan, West Germany and of course the East. Also, African governments, cautiously and nervously, would sooner take their time than rush headlong into alliances with countries hitherto quarantined and unknown to them through colonial stratagem and machinations.

In many ways the African countries, even after years of independence, find their alliance with the former imperial master indispensable. It was a reliance, a dependence, which was involuntary rather than voluntary. Bonds which, as independence was being negotiated, appeared tenuous and even worthless steadily proved as hard as steel whenever any attempt was made to drive a knife into them. In practically every department of national life, all the essential instruments—currency, education, legal system, language, press, radio, communications and scores of other apparatus which are necessary for the smooth running of government and state—had their design and even their spare parts available only or mainly in the mother country. Emotionally, too, the developmental soul of each and every one of these new countries still lay in the metropolitan country—in the churches, schools, factories, market, law courts and all other institutions.

How long these subtle ties can and will last is anyone's guess. They are there, obvious and ubiquitous, obsequious and often contradictory, effective and often elusive, unnecessary and apparently unobtrusive, experimental but often indispensable, but never altruistic so far as the imperial countries are concerned. The fact remains, nevertheless, that the earlier and the more appropriately they are fashioned to serve the very best long-term interests of these African countries and not jeopardize the content of their independence of will and of action, the better. This is the real challenge, indeed the very essence, of political independence.

One of the most potent reserves of colonialism was to focus all the attention of each colony on one particular imperial power, and to divert attention from other countries.

On the eve of his independence the African was relatively unaware of every other European country of similar weight, and severely prejudiced against the Communist world in particular. The stereotype of the Communist that had developed in the African mind was that of a wicked, uncouth and selfish atheist with a poor standard of living from whom he must take flight lest he destroy himself. It is not easy to grow out of these childish prejudices which only closer contact and personal experience can dispel, confirm or aggravate.

In the fervent desire to guard their much-treasured independence and with some knowledge of Africa's past experience, each African country views even the most benign offer from any quarter with some trepidation. The outside world, the old imperial countries in particular, are equally conscious of these morbid African fears and apprehensions. They think twice lest their intentions be misconstrued.

New connections in all fields of international cooperation crop up now and again. But the heartbeat of Euro-African relationships has always been and will always be trade. There should be no illusions whatever about this. Man, it is increasingly being said and realized, is an economic animal; this economic animal lives in a political cage.

All the frictions that can ever arise between peoples of African descent and those of European descent are precipitated in the final analysis not by racial pride, national pride, religious intolerance, cultural intolerance, etcetera, but by economic machinations, for this is the breath of life and of individual and collective security.

Again, various ties—cultural, religious, educational, military, technological, social—are all special ingredients with which the beer of economic diplomacy is brewed.

That there are certain inseparable humanitarian and friendly elements in these cooperations cannot be doubted. Even the darkest cloud has a silver lining. But altruism is a rare gesture in a ruthlessly competitive world. An element of selfishness or self-protection is usually implicit—a feeling that may perhaps belong only to the subconscious. When, for example, a technician is being trained in a host country, the international relationship is an excellent one, for it is presumed that he will return to his native country and carry certain newly acquired (the host's) influences with him. But when this technician decides to stay on, the situation changes overnight: prejudices, jealousies and deprivations of all types begin to appear. This attitude is universal and can hardly be helped—everyone wanting foreigners to act as locums so that they can be of use only for a definite period. If these locums are able to profit by their temporary status, they are simply lucky: foreigners are welcome for permanent settlement only when they become indispensable to the host group—for example, when they are used to swell manpower and population.

CHAPTER NINE

The Expediency of One Africa

In honest intentions and in practice, self-government granted to the leaders of a particular country by an imperial power can only be regarded as an installment, as part of the process whereby Africa is being gradually restored into the hands of the peoples of Africa as a whole. Otherwise self-government and independence remain a counterfeit, a mere sham. In the first place, most of these African countries are so poor and so miserably small that no one, in all honesty and providence, could possibly expect them to be viable and lead any respectable independent existence, now or ever.

Second, the new countries, even the smaller ones, are so heterogeneous that whatever bond or whatever contrivance can unite the units within themselves must also be able to unite all in that region of the continent, if not all units throughout the continent, and it should matter little whether this was under French or British or any other colonial regime. One wonders why the imperial powers, all within NATO, did not get together to set a combined plan for African independence. No one, not even the African national leaders, bothered to initiate this mode of undoing the arbitrary Berlin carving.

For any African country to logically assert to itself and to the rest of the world and to history that it is a truly independent country it will have to prove that it can be as independent of its parent country, politically, economically, culturally, as that parent country, or any other country, can ever become independent of her. Thus self-determination, national independence of action and of will, are more appropriate terms.

Indeed, independence is quite relative and is seldom if ever a complete state of affairs, nor is this necessary. We are all living in a world of interdependence, and perhaps only the United States and the Soviet Union and China can stand alone, each by itself claiming self-sufficiency and affording itself absolute independence. Even then this is a euphemism for isolationism, a less satisfying and less acceptable condition than interdependence. National self-determination must ensure national freedom and protect and promote the socio-economic and cultural life of the country from unhelpful foreign influence.

The quintessence of independence as given to the African country is political power: the instrument that must zealously strive toward the economic, cultural, military and technological autonomy of that country.

African independence must mean that Africa has the unfettered freedom to gain full control of its own destiny and to completely ensure that mistakes and crimes of yester years and yester centuries are never repeated in any color, depth or texture. In other words, Africa controlled by Africans means that African economic, agricultural and industrial development are under the complete control of the people of Africa themselves. This complete control is feasible in the modern world only through large units which have the chance, by virtue of size, population, potentiality and resourcefulness, to compete actively and fairly with those units already in existence in Europe, the Americas and Asia. But as long as old colonial demarcations continue to Balkanize African socio-economic development, Africa stands only the worst chance of attaining socio-economic independence and prosperity and would find it increasingly difficult to free itself from the pattern of trade and social development which it suffered under colonialism. The more of these countries that can coalesce to form one unit, the more feasible the attainment of autonomy in that region of the continent.

Most people everywhere are now agreed that it is only through a united African government that Africans can best express themselves in effectively securing their respectable and true independence and restoring unquestionable dignity to the people of African descent everywhere in the world. If Africa becomes a united and a strong world force, racial discrimination against Africans will prove more ridiculous and irrelevant, illusions of racial supremacy will steadily dispel themselves; the African will be able to go about his daily life anywhere in the world unmolested, no longer humiliated, no longer exploited, no longer an object of universal sympathy.

African salvation can come only through African unity, at least only through some form of common, central, effective effort, especially in the fields of economic and industrial development, trade, defense and foreign policy. The earlier this galvanized and indivisible Africa becomes a fact, the more opportunity for its salvation. Unfortunately time is very much against Africa.

Well might we ask if Africa, long subordinated, now relatively free, is merely in a remission, to be subordinated all over again, perhaps in a more permanent and inescapable way. In an age when Rome can almost be built in a day, every hour that whisks past carries with it countless and irretrievable opportunities, wealth and other unseen blessings that should belong appropriately to the peoples of the African continent.

The spirit of Africa to unite, possibly under one flag, has always been implicit in the various Pan-African deliberations held ever since the European powers decided to parcel out the continent among themselves toward the close of the nineteenth century. Happily all African leaders of this generation have publicly committed themselves to labor hard toward unity of the continent.

The sense and the logic, the expediency and the redeeming features of a united Africa are all so overwhelming, while the arguments against the continued existence of independent African states, as they are at present constituted, are equally so disarming, that, left to the ordinary African citizen, there should be no place whatever for any equivocation. A united government must be in operation immediately, this moment. It should have been already.

It is not the intention here to discuss the various dangerous and ruinous obstacles which can emerge on the way to con-

tinental unity, yet they are not insurmountable. Suffice it to
mention a few of them.

Unfortunately and inexorably, a united Africa is bound to be
severely sabotaged from within and from without, deliberately or
unwittingly, now and for a long time. Lies, fabrications, greed,
bribery and corruption, weird apprehensions, lust for power,
petty ambitions and petty jealousies—all these there certainly
must be. But all the saints would have to march on, regardless.

The willingness of contemporary African leaders to surrender
power, and how much power is to be surrendered, is the dragon
challenge that stares all and sundry in the face, the leaders themselves notwithstanding.

On the one hand, the existence of the United States and the
Soviet Union offers a challenging example and a ray of fervent
hopefulness; on the other, one sees the wilderness of a divided,
helpless and destitute Africa, with all the shame and suffering
comparable only to what obtained during the four centuries of
the Atlantic slave trade.

What type of constitutional arrangements are to be made,
federal or unitary? Is unity to commence in stages—with regional
blocs, and then, after an agreed number of years, a unified continental nation-territory?

All these are among the crucial questions to be answered by
the Pan-Africanist.

All too often, ignorant if not malicious exaggerations have
been made to multiply and amplify certain factors which apparently can block the way to continental political unity and
the comprehensive economic and industrial planning that would
definitely accrue from such an indivisible oneness of the continent. The emphasis is made that unbridgeable differences and
diversities exist throughout the continent, in race, language,
religion, culture and so on. It is being promulgated that these
would make continental political union extremely difficult if not
impossible, or even make matters worse than if the attempt were
never made at all.

Dialects have been confused with languages. Nigeria, for
example, is widely reputed to possess 248 "distinct languages,"

whereas she in fact has fewer than ten languages, which themselves are probably derived from only one or two sources.

Religious fanaticism has never been known to prevent people of different religious convictions from sharing the same cabinet table or conference hall.

With increased spread of education, and especially with popular insight into how it was possible for countries such as the Soviet Union and Japan to transform the socio-economic life of their respective countries within a generation, and the obvious prosperity and vigorousness that emerged from the political union of the fifty constituents of the United States of America under one great and powerful president as compared with their southern neighbors, who remain disunited, there is no doubt that the demand of the various peoples of Africa to be one would one day become an irrepressible reflex.

In the final analysis, education—to be equipped with essential and relevant knowledge, especially of the outside world and of the contemporary trend of international political and socio-economic development—is the sole stimulus to political consciousness and to national socio-economic opulence.

As long as any African, be he leader or follower, in any field, fails to grasp the real problems in our contemporary world and to recognize the true bearings and predicaments of Africa, he can *never* see in a proper and correct perspective the trend which African development must follow.

An initial and essential step is to set up the beacon light of African unity at Addis-Ababa. It will glow luminously for everyone, everywhere, even for those in the remotest corners of the continent to see. And such a light, with its powers, must illuminate the darkness in which millions grope.

Proper education—arousing political consciousness—is an incomparable force that will dispel or submerge the alleged centrifugal influences inherent in race, culture, religion and language throughout the continent.

Anti–Pan-Africanists assiduously insist that any attempts at African unity are doomed to result only in the exact opposite of what Pan-Africanists are setting out to achieve. They plead that attempts at unification can only meet with divergent views and internecine quarrels and that these will prove detrimental to the steady growth of each independent country as they now exist. The young states are thereby advised to retain their respective national outlooks and to jealously guard their national independence. The Anti–Pan-Africanists propose, at least by implication, that these ridiculously weak and small countries should be given every chance and every encouragement to remain, as they now are, forever independent. They are to continue building their air forces, navies, embassies and presidential palaces. They are to keep launching and relaunching their respective (thirty-eight-odd) national development plans (plans that would never get off to a start unless the countdown came from outside Africa). They are to press on with the establishment of universities and even research departments. They are also to acquire such other caricatures as will give them the delusion that, sharing the same world, they are on an equal footing with and as great, as powerful and as hopeful and secure as the United States or the Soviet Union or China or Sweden or Japan.

Anti–Pan-Africanists expect these areas of the continent to develop the infantile illusion that they are states in the modern sense because they already possess the same number of votes (one) in New York as even the superpowers and that they are at liberty to issue "strongly worded" statements on world problems. Their heads of state (rather than their representatives) can always be accorded patronizing state visits to capitals in Europe, Asia, America and other parts of the world and the VIP's of the large, powerful and populous nations can pay their patronizing visits to the little, weak, often economically destitute, thirty-eight-odd independent African countries, each one in its turn, while each visiting VIP enjoys (or is amused by) the hospitality of each of the African presidents and the enthusiasm of the yelling, waving crowds that line (or litter) the streets.

No one emergent African country can ever go it alone and play an effective independent role in the world. Any such effort can only lead to abysmal frustation and self-defeat.

The various African countries are best advised not to set

themselves the impossible task of trying to achieve individually what even far-advanced countries of Europe—those of the Free Trade Area and of the European Economic Community—are trying very hard indeed to avoid. These old autonomous and already prosperous countries are seeking their new modus operandi and their salvation in such outward-looking organizations as the E.E.C. (envisaged to lead to political unity) and its counterpart in European Communist countries.

Apologists and defeatists charge that Africa is far too heterogenous to be merged into one unit. All in all, however, Africa is far less heterogeneous than the United States or the Soviet Union.

The United States is a "heterogeneously heterogeneous" country in the sense that people from various countries and continents already within themselves heterogeneous converged to form a new country in a territory where in fact some other heterogeneous people already existed. Indeed, if Africa is racially heterogeneous by one degree, then the Americas, Australia and New Zealand are each heterogeneous by at least three degrees. The same arguments and even stronger ones would go for the cultural, religious and language diversities that serve to make up the United States and other areas of the newer world.

Again, the Soviet Union is no less heterogeneous than Africa is. It was, and still is, composed of as many different races, languages and religions as Africa today is.

If Africa, especially to the south of the Sahara, can be said to be centrifugally heterogeneous, then Nigeria alone or Gambia alone or Kenya alone can with equal force and emphasis be said to be centrifugally heterogeneous, each within itself and only to the same extent as the whole of Africa. That is to say, Nigeria is very heterogeneous, with different races, tribes, languages, religious, culture and ways of life. If Nigeria can conceivably have a way of uniting, then there must be a conceivable way of uniting an even larger block of Africa or even the whole of the African continent. If the Benin man in Southern Nigeria can share the same country with a Hausa man seven hundred miles northward, there is no earthly reason why the same Benin man should find it impossible to share the same country with the Sierra Leonean seven hundred miles westward or with the Congolese seven hundred miles southward. Furthermore, the natural resources and the taxes of this Benin man can be used to improve the lot of the Hausa, the Senegalese and the Kenyan alike.

The large size of the continent is often exaggerated as a difficulty in administration. It is true that Katanga can be better administered from Kinshasa, the Congolese capital, than from Lagos, the Nigerian capital. But it is equally true that Katanga for almost a century was effectively administered from Brussels, far away in Europe. War leaders administer their armies effectively across even two continents. The British colonial secretary only rarely visited the colonies, yet he exerted the final control over these distant lands. From the first Republic of Nigeria hundreds of Nigerian police and soldiers who had never traveled outside the capital were sent to the Congo, and they performed their duties most efficiently and got on very well with the Congolese in spite of their inability to comprehend French.

Obviously, African political and economic unity cannot be, and is not expected to be, of any economic benefit to any non-African country, especially to the countries of Europe which are at the moment Africa's main buyers and suppliers. European economic and political unity cannot be, and is not meant to be, of any economic benefit to African countries. If Europe is united economically and Africa remains disunited economically, and politically, European unity can only serve to accentuate and multiply African disunity and set African countries into open competition and even conflict among themselves. These Africans would strive only to undersell one another in Europe and elsewhere. They would thus continue to receive the worst bargain possible for their goods, as they did in previous decades and centuries.

The best and the ideal way for all and sundry is for Europe, on her own part, to unite and for Africa, on her own part, to unite. Then Europe and Africa should trade directly and unitedly with each other. Whoever unites takes all. Whoever remains disunited loses all. One only has to look at or hear of the United

States and the Soviet Unnon to be fully convinced that *union* is the magic word and the synonym for socio-economic and industrial development, no matter how you choose to spell or intonate it.

Europe, North America, Asia, etcetera, each one, have nothing whatever to lose in case of African unity except their humanitarian and magnanimous gestures; but they have everything possible and even apparently impossible to gain from African disunity. A divided and poor Africa remains a potential threat to peace throughout the world and a constant source of racial tensions and strife in many lands.

Africa has unlimited scope and incredible potentialities for achieving phenomenal socio-economic growth even within a decade, yet there are countless ways in which this transformation can be frustrated, blocked or retarded.

In 1963 the Economic Commission for Africa, after expressing deep dissatisfaction with the economic situation in Africa, concluded as follows: "Insufficient integration of national economies, the lack of diversification of production, productivity, and consequently, low income levels and inadequate savings, together with malnutrition, poor health and unsatisfactory educational level, still remains the basic characteristic in Africa."

African economies are still largely dominated by foreign monopolies. Strenuous efforts are already being made by the various governments to establish full control over their national economies. The governments are having to contend with the natural inclination of foreign enterprises to make as much profit as possible and send all such profit back to their homelands. The foreign companies are being requested to retain a substantial fraction of their profits within the territory in the best interests of the African country's development. In many instances it has become necessary to arrange 51–49 ownership of shares and distribution of profits. Foreign firms are being heavily taxed. Indusdustrial enterprises, airways, shipping lines, banks, insurance companies, newspapers, mining companies, plantations, have had to be nationalized in some of the young countries.

The world can be divided into the prosperous industralized

countries on the one hand, and on the other the underindustrialized and unindustrialized countries, which will include Greece, Portugal, southern Italy, Spain alongside the whole of Africa, except South Africa. Industrialization is the golden and indispensable key to African economic development. This statement needs qualification only to remind ourselves that healthy, well-nourished, trained people are to run the industries. Any arguments that would lead one away from the focal point of industrialization are mere charades.

In consequence, even against the advice of certain foreign countries that Africans must be patient and concentrate on agriculture, practically all governments are determined, tooth and nail, to get their countries industrialized. Light and heavy industries—iron and steel, electric power, fuel power, chemicals, insecticides—all figure prominently in their industrial plans. Like twin sisters, agriculture is to be diversified and mechanized along with industry. Substantial resources are being poured into education at all levels and for the training of technicians, scientists and engineers.

Africa is potentially one of the richest if not the richest of all continents in agricultural, mineral and certain other resources essential for economic and industrial development.

Africa is said to have the greatest water power and potential hydroelectricity in the world. There are also coal and iron ore in enormous quantities.

The U.N. and F.A.O. report on economic development in Africa, 1954–55, revealed that the continent produced 66 per cent of the world's total cocoa, 65 per cent of the palm oil, 58 per cent of the sisal, 28 per cent of the groundnuts, 14 per cent of the coffee and 11 per cent of the olive oil. It was found to be producing 96 per cent of the world's gem diamonds, 69 per cent of the cobalt, 63 per cent of the gold, 49 per cent of the antimony and 4 per cent of the iron ore, to mention a few.

An increasingly disturbing aspect of African self-government is the various cliques of exceedingly prosperous people that have emerged and are still sprouting up with the apparent liquidation of colonialism. The poorer people in some of the countries are at

least as poor as ever and have no flicker of hope that their lot
will be any better in their lifetimes. This shames every informed
African, the politicians not the least, and must disappoint all
right-thinking people the world over. This unfortunate discrep-
ancy was carried over into the new era from the high wages and
fanastic remunerations paid to European civil servants in the
colonial administration. Indigenous civil servants and the new
career politicians continue to receive these wages and remunerations, which must be astronomical, superfluous and even unjust
and immoral in the African context. Industrial houses and foreign
monopolies often offer even better attractions.

Unemployment is a complex problem. With the gross im-
balance between economic growth, that is, new jobs, and the
enormous output of new graduates and trained people, men and
women under the age of thirty-five have entered and blocked
the few available posts. They are not expected to retire for
another couple of decades or so. The queues for jobs are ever
lengthening in the face of the stampede of graduates and trained
youths from colleges inside and outside Africa.

Whereas the influence of the imperial power was manifested
through the medium of chiefs and elders, since political independence foreigners who intend to maintain their footholds
within any of these African countries have been devising new
measures and disguises to perfect their economic prowess and
perpetuate their influence. Some have "naturalized." Others have
admitted a token number of indigenous citizens into their
hierachy. The indigenous clique acts as a buffer and has only a
small or an ineffective say in the formulation of policy and in
the day-to-day running of business. Once the puppet directors
have been appointed and played patronizingly to the gallery, with
their names being given undue prominence and undue attachment to the foreign enterprise, the whole country is appeased
and everything looks good on the surface, while reassurance comes
from every direction that this is the modern way of doing things,
and the way it is done elsewhere, even in the most experienced
and prosperous countries.

The role of some of these African directors can be compared

with that of the African chiefs who were the middlemen of the slave-trade era, differing only in degree and in modernization.

Of all the economic approaches ever made to Africa since self-government commenced, none has so provoked the enlightened African and so frightened him, almost out of his wits, as the European Economic Community. It has been called collective colonialism. The European Community, acting with unity of purpose and of resources, is to trade severally with interested African states, and there is a development fund of 200 million pounds to assist economic development in the associated African states.

To many informed and thoughtful Africans the E.E.C. gesture looks not like a huge joke but like a huge Trojan horse. Suffice it to say that this looks like colonialism all over again. Although more benign in its formal and gentle approach, it yet is far more virulent and permanently crippling, and far cleverer and more attractive and tempting, than colonialism ever was. It can only jeopardize or even kill any African incentive for industrialization.

Instead of this type of economic adventure, African governments have begun to think in terms of regional free-trade areas. African continental, economic and industrial integration is being thought of. Experts are advising that certain countries should specialize in particular items of economic development in the best interests of neighboring countries.

CHAPTER TEN

The African Quintessence

Essential human needs have always been the same since Adam. These needs will never change as long as human biology, behavior and mentality remain as usual.

The basic needs of any human community are practically the same throughout the world: air, water, food, shelter and such essential services as fire fighting, light, sewage disposal and transportation.

All these necessities are as intensely human and as indispensable to the inhabitants of Ibadan in Nigeria as they are to those of Istanbul in Turkey and Melbourne in Australia and Moscow in Russia and Brazilia in Brazil and Bradford in England. Such is the parallelism that if whole populations in these places were suddenly interchanged, they would quickly avail themselves of whatever facilities are already in existence in the new localities without much fuss.

Primitivity is a subjective state. Even the most advanced country today will in certain respects be primitive by at least five hundred years in five hundred years' time. Africa today is in certain respects primitive, but only in comparison with the more developed regions of the world.

Illumination of a room, after beginning with natural light, goes on to burning oil, then burning gas, then electrical energy; and in future decades or centuries it may be atomic or some other form of power. Science can only modify the modus operandi, elaborating the means, but the end remains fixed—merely to get the room illuminated. The change in *mode* is an endless entity with profound socio-economic significance.

As long as it continues, the economies of the primitive regions, if they decide to change, and to copy as change succeeds change in the far-advanced regions, will always be helplessly tied to those of the more developed regions of the world.

But primitivity is concerned more with mode, and not with the real state (or end). To live well—as well as we can imagine and with the greatest security possible—is an end. To be what we believe we ought to be is an end. To be an African or an Asiatic or a European is an end; but perhaps to be just another human being anywhere in the world is about the greatest end.

What is of paramount importance is to ensure that each of these ends will continue to fulfill itself within the context of common humanity and within the context of interracial and international brotherhood.

A decent life essentially means a decent standard of living with normal physical and mental health, with individual and collective security and with a reliable defense against outside aggression—armed, economic or psychological.

Whereas through able leadership, discipline and realism the primitive community can continue to be contented, self-reliant and self-fulfilled, the gravest threat to it is the possibility or the occasion of armed aggression. This alone is the one and only reason that makes science and technology appear today as an absolute necessity. Obviously, the more primitive countries have lost in the arms race (perhaps it is premature to even talk of their being in it; they probably lost it before it started). The only logical step toward contentment and self-fulfillment is to concentrate on discipline, realism, self-sufficiency and profound sense of direction.

The essence of organization of human society is today very much the same as it was for our ancestors of ages past. The normal tendency is for men to live together communally, in peace, and to welcome such means as will promote peace, orderliness and efficiency. Any effort to promote the common good is known as development; it matters little whether the society is advanced or retarded. It is not surprising, therefore, that such institutions as government ministries, the civil service, diplomatic corps, the army, the police, the judiciary and local governmental bodies all meet with universal acceptability. They are all in existence or are badly needed, in one form or another, in all countries, irrespective of their political color or their stage of social advancement. These various institutions undergo continuous changes to meet the socio-economic demands and aspirations of the community. Some of them become obsolete, unhelpful or irrelevant. They are accordingly dispensed with—monarchies, chieftaincies, secret societies and so on. New ones, to meet fresh commitments, demands and experimentations, come into being: family-planning associations, old people's homes, children's homes and protective bodies, the Red Cross, banks, insurance companies, research centers, the ombudsman and such international organizations as the United Nations and allied bodies.

The highly industrialized countries of Europe and North America have attained their high standard of living and world economic dominance through their long histories as nations, the necessities and compulsions created by wars, the challenges of climate and the inescapable pressures of power politics, among other factors. Their vast economic resources give enormous impetus and buttress to research and have come to ensure that whatever is discovered or invented will be of actual economic or social benefit, enhancing national prestige and vindicating the content of an existing regime.

Most of the affluent communities and welfare states which are today commonplace in Europe and in the New World came into existence only after the First, if not the Second, World War.

The so-called developed countries are still developing and are still changing as rapidly as ever before. Older cities are being rebuilt and are expanding. Newer ones are being founded. Moreover, intensive sociological changes are taking place in all these industrialized countries. New ideas are continuously firing the aspiration of the people toward a still better life and a still more secure society. Laws and regulations governing land, crime, property and civilian life continue to undergo perceptible changes here and there. Revolutionary, deeply involved institutions, organizations, treaties (the significance of which are at times profound), continue to be thrown up into the air, and into action, all with the central aim of ensuring and consolidating collective and individual survival. Doctrines and institutions are also under palpable and constant review, all for the sake of national prosperity and security.

The general tendency is toward international cooperation among these developed countries, even in research. Joint international research institutions, collaboration and cooperation which were unutterable and unthinkable between sections of the East and the West only twenty-five years ago are already in operation: all in the common human effort to improve life on earth and to slake the unquenchable human thirst for knowledge.

Nevertheless, man's essential needs remain in essence the same; and the necessity for organizing society remains the same.

Man wants peace. He wants to live well, to live as comfortably as he can, in good mental and physical health and free from hunger, thirst, pain and discomfort, free from fear, oppression and repression. He wants to be well housed, well clothed and well protected from all dangers in his vicinity. As much as possible he wants to be self-sufficient. He wants to live long.

The introduction of science and technology has not altered man's passionate desire for these things, but his means of achieving them may have changed tremendously over the ages.

Whereas Western Europe was able with, at least in part, cheap African labor, on African soil and on American soil, and with the indispensable help of African wealth and the profiteering market in Africa, to build capital and achieve her industrial revolution, the exact opposite is true of Africa today. Africa has neither the capital nor the external markets. She now has to keep begging for capital from other continents, asking Europe, North America and Asia, as if in all altruism, to help her. African raw materials, especially agricultural resources, are increasingly being received by the richer countries with the attitude of "give it to us at this price which we think you deserve or eat it all yourself if you can." Indeed, Africa has to swim against the very waves that swept Western Europe and North America up the slippery hills of industrialization. The only probable solution to this terrible dilemma is an inward-looking, self-analytic, self-helping and self-curing developing Africa, united, with an integrated economic and industrial program. Political unity of some sort is a necessary precursor of such a unity.

Moreover, there is a new and grave real threat. Synthetic materials are being manufactured in European and North American laboratories that compete in the world market against raw materials from the developing countries.

Life in the developed countries is marked by considerable ease, convenience, comfort, safety, speed, efficiency and accuracy and with incredible dependence on the machine. In the underdeveloped countries the exact reverse is true. Life is comparatively tedious, everything is more cumbersome; there is alarming waste everywhere of almost everything, including time, brain power, manpower and natural resources. Poverty, ignorance, nakedness, chronic ill health, unemployment and beggary are all prevalent. There is incredible commitment to religion (or superstitions)—a tremendous armamentarium which insulates the mind and body from outside insults and provides a panacea for all ills. Religion would offer so much security and promise. It would alleviate pain, suffering and misery. Religion in these circumstances is a function of blind faith and ignorance rather than of rationalism or conviction.

Already practically the whole world is irrevocably committed to the continued use of the machine as a tool. Man increasingly is to make much less use of his own physical energy. He is to spend more time on leisure, entertainment, idleness and sleep. He is even to exert his brain much less—now he is merely called upon to push and press buttons and a computer delivers answers to complex calculations that would have taken hundreds of men many months a century ago. One man now does a piece of work meant for a hundred men a century ago and does it in minutes instead of months; and not only that, the finished product is of better quality and on the whole sells cheaper in the market. Man travels faster than ever before. He instantly gets news from all corners of the world. The rest of the world can be telescoped into his sitting room. There are new hazards to health which tend to shorten his life, cripple his body and afflict his mind as the tempo of development increases and more untried, man-made materials pervade his daily life. An increasing number of people, scientists included, are having recourse to the psychiatrist. It does not take an alarmist to inquire, Where is man heading? Is he already pointing a loaded gun at his own head?

Modern man owes an enormous debt to science and technology. This debt can easily be weighed in terms of his daily life, which is heavily dependent on such wonderful indispensables as his bed and linen, his cutlery, certain articles of his diet, his mode of transport, the exploration, exploitation and perfection of all matter, his means of attaining comfort, convenience and entertainment—radio, television, telephone, musical instruments, heat, light and so on—and all the means available for all sorts of personal and national defense. All these are really products of the European breakthrough into the industrial age just over a century ago. The role, indirect, remote or forced, important if not indispensable, of Africa and of Africans in achieving all these has been touched upon in earlier chapters of this book.

The incalculable debt owed to those few Europeans and Americans who, through discipline, dedication and penance, have done so very much to bring a life of greater comfort and convenience to the whole of humanity and who have given their health and their lives to this cause is a universal and eternal one. But for the fact that the human instinct is to respect all types of life and promote survival, it would have been far easier for the winners to seize all ages ago, wiping off large expanses of Asia and Africa long before there could be any ardent demands for national independence and then clearing out, for goodness' sake, from their occupied positions.

Human experience down the ages may have changed, the methods of training and of acquiring new techniques may also have changed, but there is no evidence to show that the human being has become basically wiser or brainier than his ancestors. Human capacity and potentiality seem to be fixed. Performance and achievement seem to vary with the prevailing circumstances and with the challenges inherent in environment.

Indeed, it would be inaccurate to assess the rate of economic, social and scientific development without paying due regard to the diverse forces that may have stimulated movement at a certain pace or led in a particular direction at a particular time. The United States, challenged by the Soviet Union, was able to compress a space program envisaged for ten years into a much shorter period of time. This was a sheer necessity for the United States; she was pushed into it. The pressures of cold war can be as compelling as those of real war.

But when we consider the number of universities now in existence all over the world, with the limitless facilities for education research, reference and collaboration, what turns out to be quite astonishing is not what man has been able to achieve, but what in fact has either taken him so very long to achieve or what he has not yet received or even conceived of. It often seems ridiculous that certain techniques and ideas should have eluded human thought for such a long time, that it should have taken so long an interval of time to realize that certain factors were responsible for certain things. Furthermore, with the large number of universities and their several faculties and specialities, one would expect man to have had far greater triumphs over his physical and biological environments. In fact, man ought to have been riding on his wishes already!

With the thousands of professors in the hundreds of faculties and specialities in all lands, one would expect far many more celebrated minds to have emerged: more Hippocrates', Platos, Archimedes', Shakespeares, Galileos, Newtons, Mozarts and other living legends of those earlier centuries when facilities were lamentably very limited. Nevertheless, it must be conceded that formidable frontiers are collapsing every minute before the ever-increasing and ever-invading armies of scientists, humanists and thinkers everywhere. But these breakthroughs are only seldom significant and fantastic enough to make themselves overwhelmingly revolutionary and evoke an immediate universal impact. For example, we have no device that will nourish a whole population with vitamins and proteins, or provide mass treatment.

Nor have we the literature, music or works of art that would immediately outclass the old masters and banish them from prominence or even from human want and memory!

In the West and to an increasing extent in the East there is increasing sophistication everywhere. The affluent welfare state, with greater social and material security for all, is the promise and the endeavor of every government, whatever its basic political doctrine or delineated mode of development.

Within any given society, no matter what its tint, capitalist or communist, no matter what its color or creed or its condition of material prosperity, the natural trend, the instinct, is to attempt to narrow the gap between the rich and the poor and to wipe out ignorance. The trend is to introduce as much freedom of speech, justice and fair play as will at least improve the image of the country abroad, in a smaller world where little can be hidden, gagged or tranquilized. Everyone, from granny to toddler, sees, feels and believes that this is the best thing. Only the platitudes of vanity, selfishness and insecurity would lead them away from this vein of thinking. Indeed, most governments genuinely mean well for their citizens. Most governments mean to be good. Most of them mean to be effective, humane, realistic, fair and just. But all too often governments find themselves unable to accomplish these liberal ideals, for one reason or another.

At any given time, and in any given place, man desires, rather than requires, first for himself and then for his family circle, then for his kith and kin, the highest standard of living he has seen, heard of or imagines to be possible. But in his realism he appreciates that even though he may wish and desire, it does not mean he should always go out of his way to suffer or to defeat himself unnecessarily and foolishly.

Ignorance has its main redeeming feature in the fact that a person can remain quite happy and contented with his lot if he is ignorant of anything better, or if he is so ignorant as to believe that he cannot possibly have it any better. This is the situation today, first, in the most advanced societies in the world, and second, among the ignorant people in developing countries.

Provided the members of a community are in good health, without pain or hunger, provided there is no visible threat to their freedom and collective dignity, and provided they are protected and armed against the various dangers of life in their environment, they certainly will live a happy and contented life.

Contentment is not synonymous with complacency. The community continues to develop as new challenges crop up: new threats, population growth, all sorts of fulfillments and ambitions, and the almost irresistible craving for something better, cheaper, quicker, more efficient, easier.

There are those who feel contented because they believe, even if wrongly, that anything better than what they already have is certainly beyond their reach, for reasons best known to them; they remain contented as long as they feel sure in themselves that they are not being cheated, cajoled or exploited by any outsiders.

It is also possible that certain peoples derive enormous physical, mental and spiritual strength and contentment from their religion or other beliefs (which outsiders might dismiss as superstitions). But these peoples invariably stand to be materially cheated and robbed by others who sagaciously lay all emphasis on material life.

Science and technology only improve and elaborate the modus operandi; basic human necessities cannot be altered. The introduction of science and technology into human consciousness is no more of a threat to Africanism than it is to Europeanism or Americanism or humanism. Apart from altering the modus operandi, science and technology together form a dispensable entity; the human being can do without them.

The demand for science and technology and the difficulty of dissociating them from European and American economy and culture certainly predispose the African to economic and cultural domination from these continents. European scientific, economic and cultural domination over the African will surely lead to social domination. Social domination in this wise is a root cause of racial discrimination, racial bigotry and unrest throughout the world.

Whether cultures, climates, colors, creeds and other factors in the human background are different for the sake of beauty, variety and completeness or for the sake of difference, confusion and separateness is a moot point. In any case I am different from you because I am already preconditioned or even predestined not to be you, and because you do not have to be me. Even though we may be the same, we are still separate entities. Because we always have been, and because we both still are in existence, it means we can still continue to co-exist and to co-persist, however precariously.

It is patently part of my dignity to speak in a tongue and with style, accent and even gesticulations that are distinctively mine. These may even characterize me. They probably reflect, and re-call to me, the memories and glories of my ancestors, of whom I may be very proud and whose presence I want always to be able to re-create or reincarnate. They are irreplaceable; I want them perpetuated. I do not want, in my quest for a better life, to keep being like you in every way: learning, thinking and hearing about you always, and wanting to be essentially like you. I do not want to replace the memories, the greatest glories or even the most horrible woes of my ancestors and the heroes of my people with yours. I like to be with you and would like you to be with me, but I do not believe anything will be gained by my being exactly like you simply because I want to continue to be. If I should need to be exactly like you in order to be at all, then I really do not deserve to be, and do not deserve to be reckoned with. In this wise I must be a thorough letdown to humanity and a disappointing failure to my ancestors.

But I cannot reject what I am convinced is really good just because I feel it did not belong to me originally. Nothing derived solely from my own ancestors alone. My own ancestors are too vague to belong to me alone. Everything derived from *our* ancestors. Yet certain things do belong to you or to me more than they belong to me or to you, and these automatically, con-sciously or subconsciously, form part of our inner pride or humility.

Again, what is really good is always really good. Few things are really good. Mozart is good and adorable but only at most places and only at most times. Picasso enjoys universal fame in the sense that he is known by that part of the universe which recognizes and remains attentive to him; those not so privileged or so unfortunate do not have to draw like Picasso or play like Beethoven in order to enjoy real fulfillment as regards universal fame. And what of Chandra, Cheng or Chigbo?

The fact that things are *different,* in so far as they express different human experiences and different backgrounds and strive to reflect things hitherto unknown—this alone makes them good and worth treasuring.

To the African in inexorable and inescapable contact with Western civilization, through newspapers, radio and screen, the highest standard of living he knows is that found in Europe and North America. It is the natural tendency or an obvious temptation for him to attain this luxurious living. If possible, he would emigrate there, or import wholesale European or North American social and welfare amenities and even wealth onto the African soil.

Here is Africa only recently escaped from the darkness of the slave trade and latterly from European colonization of Africa into the dazzling, blinding sunshine of Western civilization. How should Africa develop with this fabulous wealth, exuberance and the highest standard of living ever seen by or known to man on earth so near to her shores?

The African must, in the light of his background, the evidences that surround him and the signs that stand prominently ahead, develop or discover his own values and his own ideals.

Must the African be encouraged to seek, or must he of necessity seek, the same material ends in life as the European or the American or the Chinese? Must he endeavor to attain or cultivate the same criteria or fashions for his comforts, conveniences, leisures and fulfillments as they do in other continents, even in spite of his different background? Needless to say, this background of the African is strikingly different from what obtains in other continents in terms of stage of social advancement, in terms of economic resourcefulness and possibilities, in terms of history, geography, culture, race, religion, climate and other factors.

It is crystal clear that as long as he seeks exactly the same ends as the European or the North American, the only chance the African has is that of being a perpetual trailer. He will never come into his own socially, culturally, politically or economically. He will never be truly fulfilled in himself.

If Africa must have a breakthrough, it will not and it cannot be into science and technology as we already know these to be and in which it is already hopelessly left behind. It might be through a different frontier from Europe's, or through a different point on the same frontier, into a new era in Africa (and in the world) in which the quintessence of the African would reign supreme.

How, then, can the African now seek and attain something out of this life to give him an end worth fighting for—to give him satisfaction, self-respect, self-fulfillment, universal respect and a promising continuity? What is the end purpose of African development? What is the realistic way of achieving it? What must be the real *meaning* and the *ultimate objective* of "development" for the African?

While the most sophisticated areas of Europe and North America are struggling desperately to avoid getting themselves enslaved by the machines they are inventing, Africans are struggling hard not to be culturally, economically and socially enslaved by the foreign patterns of life they are importing in their enthusiasm for a better life. How can Africa develop without being over-Europeanized or over-Americanized or over-Asianized?

Science and technology and socio-economic development in Africa are aspiring to follow the patterns set in the far-advanced countries. Science and technology both constitute a threat to the African personality, although still capable of invigorating it. But as things are in mid-twentieth century, the more scientific and technological innovations that intrude themselves into the African consciousness, the greater the depletion of, or the challenge to, the African personality, in so far as European culture, especially European languages, forms the vehicle for these innovations.

Only a specially distilled social philosophy that vividly recognizes those things which are quintessential for the African and that would cherish these and allow science and technology to promote them can save the African from the dangers inherent in an increasingly wealthy and small world.

Far and away the greatest desire of the African is happiness and contentment which is well founded. The *quintessence* of life for the African is that life should prove, now and for all times, to be full, satisfying, real, enviable, respectable and reasonable and never pretentious, illusory, fastidious, ridiculous, despicable or pitiable. The African is to live in excellent physical health and live for as long as possible. He is to live in excellent mental health and live for as long as possible. He is to live in peace, without fear of physical destruction from inside or outside his own continent. He is to live in peace without fear of a psychological defeat. He is to be able to live alone, self-reliant and self-sufficient, and he is to be able to live with all, from within or without his continent. He is to live in freedom and dignity, and this essentially means not economically subservient to any foreign power. He is to live as comfortably and as conveniently as possible, but only within his own means and only according to his own resources—in the African environment. He is to live a life that places great premium on simplicity on its road to perfection and relies more on the natural than on the artificial—a life that uses machines to develop the African as a personality in the world rather than to destroy his identity, undermine his dignity, stifle his soul or destroy his human reverence. He is excessively conscious of the heritage he will bequeathe to his posterity.

The quintessence is to attain and maintain a life of contentment and happiness for the ordinary African, such that he will live in brotherly neighborliness with his fellow men free of envy, slander and calumny. It is not only the contentment and happiness of the educated elite, the civil servants, politicians, wage earners and businessmen alone—if these vigorously awakened people can in themselves ever again achieve contentment from their feeling of belonging materially to the same world of materialism as the people in far-advanced countries. The ordinary African must be psychologically protected from the tormenting and tantalizing shadows and mirages of a material life he hardly needs, a life he can hardly attain, at least for the moment, lest it be one of economic, cultural and even moral bankruptcy.

The case for being exquisitely conscious of an African quintessence in the modern world will be adduced from the following premises: It is overwhelmingly obvious that Africa today is grossly underdeveloped economically in comparison with practically all the rest of the world. The standard of living in Africa is desperately low, annual income per capita in most parts being less than 35 pounds, while in Western Europe the figure is around 480 pounds and in the United States it is said to be about 560 pounds. The basic human needs in Europe and in Africa remain essentially the same, and the peoples of Europe, America and Africa are paradoxically and cruelly subject to the same international dollar and gold. All of them are obliged to trade in the same market. The various countries and their citizens are often free to buy whatever they wish, all of them, from the same markets.

For a long time and especially since political independence, the leaders and people of some of the developing countries have striven assiduously to convince the world (they have in fact been deceiving themselves) that they can well afford what in fact they can at best only ill afford. They have been importing artificial oases of wealth into their dismal deserts of poverty: displaying their national airlines, navies, chancelleries, presidential palaces, Rolls-Royces, fabulous hotels, etcetera. Professional and personal attire, insigna and medallions and other paraphernalia complete the picture of the schizophrenic African living in his little world of make-believe. Consumer goods of every description are in incredible abundance, as in any big store of Europe or North America. The foreigner in parts of Africa is astounded to find everything she needs within arm's length, from Parisian perfumes to Canadian fur coats. Indeed, not until she steps out into the scorching sunshine of Africa from the air-conditioned store is she reawakened from this dreamland to the fact that the store is not in Brisbane, Bonn or Boston but in an African capital city. This is hardly a credit to the African city! What of the slums a few yards away, the foul-smelling open drainage, the horrible sewage-disposal system in the house next door and the scores of pitiable rag-clad, blind, crippled beggars at the entrances of this large ultramodern store? What of the malnourished and hungry faces rushing to give a generous helping hand to transfer the goods into the immaculate sports car standing in the muddy parking lot?

Apologists, defeatists and foreign economists can argue at length that this is the standard pattern for any country that must develop. But it cannot be a credit to the African city in point; at best it portrays the social injustice and callousness inherent in the place.

The existence of these deep pockets of wealth in huge robes of rags cannot be difficult to explain. It all began during the era of colonialism. The purpose then was to import Europe into Africa and export Africa into Europe and for Europeans to occupy and rule Africa. The continued trend, with foreign consumer goods innundating the daily lives of Africans, is an unmistakable hangover from colonialism, if not an addiction to it.

The first cardinal step toward real African economic independence and self-determination for a better life is a clean, clear and determined break with the past; to live and consume rationally and realistically as Africans of this generation should; to earn money as Africans of this generation should, and not as European administrators and civil servants tended to earn during the colonial era or what they would have continued to earn had colonialism not been more or less liquidated. The African toddler must first remove its tiny feet from the huge shoes imported and left behind by colonialism; only after this can it really crawl, walk and then run.

Again, has slavery stopped or has it merely changed in character and disposition to attune itself to the conscience and circumstances of our age? It is common knowledge that in most African countries, after political independence was achieved, the governments merely allowed the indigenous Africans to step into the shoes of their European predecessors, to enjoy all the remunerations of office. Of particular significance is the ownership of imported cars by young civil servants. These cars are bought on loans provided by the African government, and maintenance costs are met in addition. The African youth is thus forced by these circumstances to expend a handsome fraction of his sweat and toil to meet the cost of the car by regularly repaying the government loan, and this money ultimately finds its way into industrial houses in far-distant lands. By the time this young man finishes the payment of this loan, with the shattering condition of roads and the high cost of car servicing in Africa, it is high time for a new car. It is obvious that the energies of this youth go into laboring, foolishly, to feed the market in other lands, where his car was manufactured. Quite often he spends well over half his earnings on the maintenance of this machine whose spare parts, and even the soap required for washing, are available only from the outside world. Instead of bus fare costing him a shilling, he has to give up ten shillings, excluding the inevitable wear and tear on the car. He enjoys all the luxuries of a five-seater all by himself, doing over 90 per cent of 20,000 miles sitting alone, riding solo, at times with the back seat almost untouched until the car is ready for replacement.

Indeed, it is inconceivable that certain European countries, in spite of their long history and their higher standards of living, have far fewer private cars altogether than certain African countries have in their national capital alone, all within a decade. It is also inconceivable that the European countries which many of their former colonies tend to emulate never accord "privileges" to their young civil servants similar to what various African governments tend to accord to theirs. The argument bandied about is that African countries have not got adequate public-transport facilities and that the roads are bad—an argument that evaporates at the touch of questioning. If the roads are too bad to carry big buses, they must be worse still for saloon cars. If public transport is inadequate or inefficient, in what sense are private cars adequate or efficient?

The most ridiculous addition to this is the hire-purchase system for luxuries which is in operation in many African countries in exactly the same way as in the far-advanced, prosperous countries.

Poverty is still prevalent in practically all countries of the world, including the United States. All countries are striving very hard to wash their dirty linen at home and solve their problems of poverty and social discontent in their own way. They often have to bear in mind their respective national histories, resources and consciences, and also their national images in the world at large.

The far-advanced countries do show sympathetic and humane attitude to African "secondary" poverty by giving large amounts of their capital and other hard-earned resources to develop one of the richest of the continents.

The richer countries continue to allow their volunteer workers and missionaries, in their endless trickle, into Africa, to comfort, cure and convince Africans, even at the risk of their lives. All these humanitarian efforts cannot be expected to continue to come to Africa forever, for the same purposes. It is as immoral as it is unfair to expect them to do so. There must come a time when they will have to stop, or even reverse; otherwise a perpetual breadwinner-dependent relationship will emerge. Such a relationship would always constitute an embarrassment to an Africa that wants to preserve its dignity and self-respect.

The earlier the developing countries achieve self-sufficiency, especially as regards food production and essential services, the better for the whole of mankind. All development programs must therefore be geared to provide food and the essential services in the developing countries.

But another essential need must be satisfied. It is no secret that the poor nations cannot defend themselves. They are insecure as long as they cannot arm themselves by themselves, and in a practical way. As such it pays them best to exploit the human instinct for peace and work for peace and good will everywhere.

The African in his faithful, virtuous and legitimate search for freedom and liberty groaned under the yoke of slavery and colonialism. He now continues to moan and groan, and wonders whether foreign slavery and colonialism have not been exchanged for indigenous slavery of another texture or tone, perpetrated by a privileged segment of society and perhaps with the aid and abetment of outside influences.

Far less than a thousandth of the population in Africa can possibly attain in this generation the present Western and Eastern European standard of living. The neglible fraction of Africans who could possibly attain that standard can hardly do so without exploiting the rest of their own people—their labors, ignorance or misfortune.

This privileged class of Africans cannot enjoy their high standard of living without the benefit of certain advantageous relationships with special outside influences either in their own name or in the name of their people. They may have been awarded local or foreign scholarships to receive their education from public funds collected locally or granted to them from abroad, not as individuals but only as representatives of the teeming millions of their countrymen. They may have received government loans from public funds to build their capital investments. Ostensibly they were the ones who had the requisite "security," and public money would be lent to them on this score. They may have been professing to represent the interest of some of their own people—for example, doing humanitarian work, building schools, workshops, hospitals or factories to serve the vast numbers of suffering and miserable Africans whose welfare they would proclaim to a susceptible and sympathetic outside world.

The African after political independence must be reborn to think again and to develop a new intelligent and realistic sense of values of his own. This renascent African must be able to know exactly when he must admire, pooh-pooh or ignore the exuberances and excesses of a world outside his own context.

If the peoples of Africa can have their own distinctive values, if they can define for themselves their own needs and adhere to these, if they can know exactly when their peoples have been well fed, well housed, well clothed, well adorned, well entertained—being fully conscious of what they need as a people and what they can best afford from their own resources and reserves —they are likely to feel happy and contented and accept their lot as their lot and they can then surge forward together as a nation. But if they hope or their circumstances are such that they can hope or be encouraged to hope, as individuals or as nations, to reach for the standards created outside their own world and to shop in exactly the same way, and in exactly the same markets, and with the same sense of priorities, as the citizens of the far-advanced countries, they will do so only to their own eternal detriment and frustration.

A most essential step, therefore, in bringing happiness and contentment to the African in an ever-shrinking, rich and materialistic world is to know how much of the materialism and ambition of the richer countries he requires to inject into his daily life and into his national life to make these not only real and full for himself but fuller and even more secure and meaningful for his own posterity.

Does the African, educated or illiterate, need to have vodka or whisky for alcohol, a tail coat for his wedding, a Persian carpet for his floor, a golden wrist watch to keep time, a diamond tiara for a necklace, a private car to move from one place to another, a private transistor to hear news from across oceans and lands? Does he really need imported films, starring foreign actors and actresses, and foreign pop music for his entertainment?

In the African quintessence the individual must be persuaded or made to live and to possess only according to the prevalent national means and standards. This is about the only road to general contentment with the material life in a given environment.

The most expensive things in the world market, if not the best of everything in our material life today, are found in the far-advanced countries of Europe and North America: food—from pure water and sweets to brandy and steak; machines —from toys and pens to trucks, aircraft and oceangoing ships; furniture—from foot mat to golden bed; ornaments—from imitation earrings to rare gems and gold-embroidered garments.

There is no hope whatever, at the moment or in the foreseeable future, that materials produced in Africa (with all the machines that have to be imported for the purpose) will be able to match in quality those produced in the far-advanced countries. Those produced locally must be given fool-proof and "advertisement-proof" protection. As long as the citizens of a developing country are allowed to possess just any types of commodities simply because they are in fashion in the far-advanced countries, irrespective of whether these are mere luxuries or absolute necessities (even though the government of the developing country may believe they can curb or discourage their importation by levying prohibitively high taxes), the citizens of the developing country cannot be easily dissuaded from buying these non-essentials. These citizens, including those in the high-income group, are cruelly exposed to irresistible materialism, rendered even more compulsive by superb advertising. Without anyone coming to their rescue, their appetites continue to grow with consumption, while their pockets and their security dry up. They remain indefinitely a fastidious and discontented lot. The national economy continues to be crippled by this unfortunate exchange of their limited hard-earned resources for luxuries in preference to those items which are absolutely necessary for healthy growth.

It is very doubtful whether the usual attempts to curb wealth and to prevent the illicit entry and dumping of foreign goods into a country would be enough for socio-economic development in Africa. There must be very tight control. The African environment must be such that the individual is forced, exhorted or persuaded to help in building up national capital and to invest his money in a way that will benefit the national economy and consolidate the essential needs of the whole population.

As long as African social development, African individual

social needs and the wealth of the African are encouraged to
remain exactly the same in detail, quality and quantity, as long
as things can be acquired in the same way and exhibited and
utilized in the same way as in the far-advanced countries, Europe
and North America (and the other more advanced countries)
will have everything to gain while African countries have a
great deal to lose.

Africans who have become privileged should not endeavor,
and should not even be allowed, to keep up with the Joneses of
Munich, Manila, Moscow, Milwaukee or Melbourne; rather, they
must continue to live with their own people, helping them. They
must appreciate that the Joneses they are to keep up with, in a
progressive way, are those next door. These are the Joneses with
whom they share a common history and background and also a
common posterity and destiny. These are the people they can
help and advise so that the great era will emerge, in the not
distant future, when any African Jones can live as happy and
contented a life as any Jones of Europe or America or parts of
Asia lives in his land.

The citizens of a developing country, before they can truly
emerge from their economic doldrums, must first undergo a
period of strict governmental control, vigorous national discipline,
individual self-denial and self-restraint, and patriotic cooperation. Indeed, they must undergo a period of hardship during
which they can build up the momentum for their economic take-
off. They will need to develop tremendous resistance against
European, Asiatic and American goods—goods of unending
quality and increasing quantity, and even easy market value,
which incessantly bombard their shores. The public cannot be
relied upon to do this voluntarily. There needs must be strict
government control throughout this period of determined and
calculated austerity.

Where discipline stops, and curtailment of freedom and
liberty begins, is a fad for the tyro. No doubt voices of all kinds,
of all motivations, would be heard from inside and outside the
continent which could only confuse the citizens of Africa about
the sanity or sanctity of measures such as these.

The education of the public as regards the purposes and honest intentions of this self-restraint is equally essential.

Very few Africans bother, or indeed need bother, about the scientific theories and definitions of socialism as recognized in other parts of the world. These presumably suit the areas concerned. Most Africans should be guided more by what they believe to be fair and realistic; they should be guided by what they are convinced is a pragmatic and practicable approach to their own problems.

Be that as it may, it is remarkable that both capitalism, as known in the West, and Communism, as known in the East, have mellowed considerably since the last world war. They are no longer the irreconcilable extremes they used to be. All evidences point to more compromises and revisions being made on both sides. Capitalism and Communism are both steadily becoming more and more humane, realistic, fair and just to all segments of society. Both of them seem in recent years to be gaining a more vivid insight into human nature. The arguments for operating with private capital are often as convincing as those for state ownership and a planned national economy. Encouraging enterprise and incentiveness is as urgent and desirable as discouraging nonchalance and irresponsibility.

Socialism, as held in most places, cannot be a complete answer to development, however well-meaning its advocates may be. It cannot be successful without severe discipline, rigid legislation and a dedicated leadership irrevocably committed to what it believes to be best for the present and for the future. For the leadership to be successful, it must be capable of carrying the people along with it and of enlisting their cooperation willingly or by force, at times by brutal force.

Capitalism in Africa is inherently a suspect and unfair system. There is no doubt that capitalism encourages enterprise, efficiency, devotion and fulfillment of self or group. Capitalism requires a degree of competitiveness and even heartlessness. It plays upon all types of human susceptibility. It is a real struggle for survival perhaps too extraordinary for anyone's true comfort. It can be quite ruthless, selfish and oppressive. If social justice, or equal creative opportunity for all citizens, is the national objective, capitalism can never achieve it; in fact, it probably will do the opposite.

Whereas in North America and Europe capitalism may be justified in terms of the true venturesomeness, heroism and boldness of enterprise in the New World that built it up, in Africa (and for Africans), on the other hand, the situation is entirely different. Any advantage in amassing any sizable capital after the departure of slavery and colonialism can often be traced to opportunism of some sort, for example importation of foreign capital, granting of government loans, nepotism, bribery and corruption.

Colonialism did not precondition any person or any family to wealth. Any wealth that exists is built up or sustained with the aid of the new government by providing loans and providing such an atmosphere as will encourage business to flourish. When all is said and done, the rich man, anywhere, is infinitely obligated (and indeed, partly owes his wealth) to the forces that maintain the peace and to those that maintain law and order in his neighborhood. The poor man usually has little or nothing to lose, except perhaps his poverty.

The African elite have demanded self-govenrment in the name of their people and for the best interests of the whole people, not for the elite themselves or for any other segment of the population in particular. Indeed, colonialism has already helped in preconditioning independent African countries to some form of socialism.

If African rich can suffer African poor, then, within the context of the same humanity, there is no reason to expect that Europe will not have the heart to continue to coexist with and yet oppress, suppress and exploit Africa and develop at the expense of Africa and even enslave Africa. If people cannot be persuaded to show charity toward their own countrymen, it would be rather much to expect foreigners to show charity, freely and unreservedly.

Again, if the argument were that in any given country there must always be classes, merely because classes always existed,

even though we hold that all are potentially equal, then the tenet
of a superior race would hold good: the European race should be
accepted, as a matter of everlasting fact, to have been accorded
divine selection, merely because, so far, in our own age, certain
members of this race have proved intellectual leadership by their
achievements in certain important aspects of human development.

There is every cogent reason to believe that pragmatic austerity in developing countries, inspired and executed by the citizens
themselves and applied to natives and foreigners alike, is a prerequisite for breaking loose from the colonial socio-economic
meshwork in these areas. To believe that it is already too late
to redeem the present socio-economic trend in Africa, a liability
established during the colonial era, is the first breath in admitting
that colonialism will never end in its substance, that Africa will
never truly recover from colonialism and that Africa will never
acquire the necessary capital for its development.

The emphasis in developing countries must be on *economy*
in the simple and true sense of the word. The keynote must
always be *austerity*, rather than squandermania for personal
luxuries and prestigious national projects. Imported products,
especially machines, must be savagely curtailed, and those which
are allowed entry must be available mainly for communal use,
for the maximum number of people possible, with indigenes and
foreigners all in the same boat.

Well might we ask, What is the purpose of international
trade? The essence of favorable international trade is for nations
to buy whatever they believe they really need for their socio-
economic and even cultural advancement but which, unfortunately and incidentally, they cannot get at home, presently or
soon, to serve the purpose. Ideally the goods imported must be
of definite benefit. They must promote the best interests of the
nation in a specific way, economically, morally or culturally.
They must improve the well-being of the individual and the
community as a whole, presently and for all time. The purpose
of trade is not merely to displace local material—a fatal thing to
do—but rather to render these more efficient, effective or relevant

in over-all planned national development. The ultimate aim is a balance that augurs well for self-sufficiency. The nation continues to import and to export until it is able to provide itself with the sort of goods it has been importing or until it is able to find suitable substitutes locally to fulfill the same needs and functions in the economic fabric of the nation. A robust and thriving internal market allows for self-sufficiency. This then promotes greater export; it invigorates the internal market and improves the general standard of living of the people.

If, after political independence, Africa's new *assimilados* continue to crave ardently, perhaps in their addiction or in their pitiable susceptibility to the standards, values, luxuries, machines and other foreign goods which the European colonialist would have brought with him into Africa anyway had colonialism not been liquidated, then, in essence, colonialism is neither invalidated, dead nor buried. At best the ordinary African peasant has been safely returned to square one, but with a different and perhaps more intractable group of middlemen, formed this time by Africa's new *assimilados*.

Imported wealth and imported poverty, almost equally, have their inimical influences on the host community, depending on circumstances. Poverty invariably lowers pre-existing standards, but expensive personal belongings tend to engender new feelings of greed, acquisitiveness and social instability, seducing morality into jeopardy.

Usually the entry of poverty, disease and unemployment is vigorously controlled in every country by stringent immigration laws, special concessions being made only in the case of refugees from persecution and such natural disasters as floods and earthquakes. In exactly the same way, wealth can sometimes constitute a disease, at least in a psychological sense, in an environment where hitherto such wealth was never known or seen by a people who were reasonably content and happy with what they already had. If new wealth is in a form that contributes to the over-all improvement of the people's lot as a whole, for example by improving their social and welfare amenities, this will be of obvious benefit. But where the wealth merely amounts to an exhibition of some luxurious foreign standard, for example, expensive personal radio, camera, helicopter, gold-plated car, bicycle, yacht, suit, furniture, liquor or other acquisition, then this will merely create new fastidiousness and fresh hopelessness. It will sometimes represent a new challenge, indeed a new curse on the people.

It would be far better for Africa to keep exporting all its diamonds and gold to those in the richer countries who need them for purposes best known to them in exchange for hard cash and for those materials which are indispensable in planned socio-economic growth and in improving the general standard of living of the peoples of Africa.

No attempt need be made to discourage the African from seeing, hearing and even receiving part of his inspiration from the traditions, ways of life, scientific and technological advancements, of other parts of the world. But physical contact of the African with these foreign influences on the African soil must be selective and guarded.

The African would like to see thousands of foreigners coming to trade, help, visit or settle in Africa, but it must be considered unnecessary for these friends of Africa to bring with them just about any forms of their riches to which they were so used in their own environment and to introduce these into poor and miserable African environments.

Just as yellow fever, smallpox and typhoid fever are endemic in African countries and foreigners must get themselves immunized against these diseases, so is poverty a major endemic social terror that haunts the African continent at the moment, and all foreigners must be prepared to sympathize with this, not only by giving aids, loans and grants but also by helping to keep their excesses back in their home countries. They must immunize themselves against poverty and accept living with the African as the African should really and truly live at this stage of socio-economic development of the continent.

Presumably, these foreign friends enter the continent to live *with* Africans and not *on top of* them, to help, and not to dramatize to them how glamorous life can be elsewhere.

Just as the African is so poor that he cannot go into the far-advanced countries to study unless on an African grant or a foreign grant, with enough dollars, pounds or francs to meet the high cost of living before he is allowed entry or even before he is allowed to leave his country, so must it be that unless the man from a far-advanced country will make some token sacrifice, shedding his golden coat of mineral wealth, he should not be allowed entry into the African continent. He cannot, in such a desperately poor environment, expect to enjoy the high standards that he left behind at home. If such standards were in existence in Africa, they would be confined either to 0.01 per cent of the native population or to inhabitants who are non-Africans. The rest of the population would then be obliged to stand aghast and marvel at the fantastic wealth which they can never have. These Africans would remain chattels, they would be second-class citizens, and could not actually be masters in their own home.

Whereas it is only in the name of freedom and liberty that the African can attain contentment, happiness and a promising continuity, it is also in the name of freedom and liberty that he would continue to wallow and groan in discontentment, misery and depersonalization, having sold out to the materialism of the outside world.

The real crisis in Africa is one of individual and national awareness and purposefulness. There must be adequate knowledge and understanding of all the issues at stake. Until Africans are adequately informed and oriented, until they can properly understand the issues at stake, until they are able to distill for themselves what things are quintessential for their well-being, they can never appreciate the true meaning, the limits and the limitations of freedom and liberty. The contentment and happiness of themselves and of their posterity would on this score remain quite questionable in every respect.

The key to African development is the very stimulus to African consciousness. This key and the stimulus are to be found in mass education, deliberate and purposeful.

The new Africa owes it as a primary and bounden duty to

humanity at large to rise up to such logical and reasonable standards as will make the concept of universal human brotherhood tenable. Other peoples must neither be exposed by Africa to temptation, nor must their indifference or humanitarianism be alienated. Africa in remission, rather than allowing history to repeat itself, perhaps in an entirely different manner, must brazen itself up and multiply its thinking a hundredfold so as to catch up with the rest of humanity.

The emphasis in human survival has shifted from arms races and warfare to a new kind of war—a war of brains, of nerves, of sight and foresight.

If the present generation of Africans who have already lost the race, or have had it lost for them, are unable, with all their conscience, consciousness and prescience, to book now a respectable place for their posterity, then they will have failed incalculably. Indeed, the best role and the greatest fulfillment of the present generation of Africans lies in ensuring that they will achieve a definite breakthrough into this respectable African future before it becomes much later; otherwise the opportunity will never again return.

In all human history the leadership of a people has never been so vital in shaping the destiny of posterity as it is today in Africa, where practically every move by any government is bound to be appreciably influenced by foreign presence, influence and experience, and even by foreign capital.